SAVING TRAPPERS LAKE

The Shannondale Crew, 1955

This is the earliest photo of the author—second one from the left—as a young man, going on eighteen at the time. The boy on the right is Darrel Scarff, the author's friend from Burlington, Iowa, the author's home town. See Chapter One. The names of the other two are lost to history.

SAVING TRAPPERS LAKE

And other adventures of a Forest Ranger

A memoir of my career in the US Forest Service

jim hagemeier

This book was composed in Microsoft Word, formatted with Microsoft Publisher, and printed to PDF with Adobe Acrobat DC. Final print copies were made from the PDF file. Microsoft is a registered trademark of the Microsoft Corporation. Adobe and Acrobat are registered trademarks of Adobe Incorporated.

Cover photo by Bradleyboulder at the English Wikipedia [GFDL (http://www.gnu.org/copyleft/fdl.html)
or CC-BY-SA-3.0 (http://creativecommons.org/licenses/by-sa/3.0/)]

Black and white edition (all interior color illustrations have been converted to shades of gray)

Published by James L. Hagemeier
Printed on 60-pound archival paper for longevity.
Made in the United States of America.

ISBN 978-1-7338121-1-5

Table of Contents

ACKNOWLEDGEMENTS

Thanks to daughter Heidi Hagemeier who inspired me to write this memoir and as a journalist did the editing. Also, many thanks to my neighbor at our winter home in Tucson, Arizona, Kristin Delaplane, who teaches classes on oral history and story-telling. She helped me organize, document, and publish my book.

Also, thanks to several individuals who allowed me to use their photos: Mike McMillan, owner of Spotfire Images, for photos of a smokejumper at the start of Chapter 3 and for the fire photo at the start of Chapter 8. Roger Savage for the photo of the crew at Moose Creek, Idaho, in Chapter 3, and the Mann Gulch Memorial photo in Chapter 19. JB Stone for the photo of a fire fighter in Chapter 3. Jason LaBelle, Director of the Center for Mountain and Plains Archaeology, Colorado State University, for the Rollins Pass photo in Chapter 9. The National Smokejumpers Association for the logo on the Chapter 3 title page.

I sought help in reconstructing events involving Trappers Lake in Colorado. First to Tom Thompson, a former Forest Service employee, who provided me with information on Forest Service management direction when I worked on my planning and design work at Trappers Lake in 1962. I also got help from the Forest History Society located at Duke University in Durham, North Carolina. They researched and found the 1929 maps and management direction for the Trappers Lake vicinity proposed by the Forest Service for the establishment of the Flattops Primitive Area that was designated in 1934. I also got insights into the involvement of Arthur Carhart in fostering the establishment of Wilderness Areas from Matthew Pearce, who wrote the article "Cradle of the Wilderness, part 1, 2016" celebrating the passage of the Wilderness Act of 1964. And a special thank you to Tom Wolf who authored the book *Arthur Carhart: Wilderness Prophet*, who spent time discussing Arthur Carhart's life and his own experiences at Trappers Lake with his father at about the same time I was working there. Thanks to the National Forest Museum of Forest Service History that supported my effort by publishing my story on Trappers Lake in their newsletter and produced the map in Chapter 5.

Thanks also to my wife, Gretchen, who did a last-minute proof-reading that substantially improved the quality of the final product. Her experience as an English teacher proved to be very helpful.

Lastly, I would like to express my appreciation to G. David Thayer of Rapidsoft Press LLC, for doing the final editing of my book and formatting it for publication. Without his expertise, I would never have been able to make this happen. I felt like an absolute beginner in all aspects. His patience in explaining everything was outstanding. Huge thanks to David. I felt like I had met a brother. We both hiked the same mountains in Colorado and shared the same interests in life.

INTRODUCTION

I am now in my twilight years. I've had a good life and feel blessed. My career spanned thirty-five years, all with the U.S. Forest Service. I always thought I lucked out working for the Forest Service. It's a remarkable agency. It has a mission that protects national treasures while providing the public with opportunities to use many and varied resource values. I never thought of myself as a government employee and frankly would not have worked for another agency. I spent time in the U.S. Army, but I was prouder of serving my nation as a forest ranger. I started as a firefighter, was hired as a landscape architect, and became a forester.

I was hired full time by the Forest Service in 1961 after working for them part time for six summers. Up until that time the organization was primarily made up of foresters. They were noted to be able to fill most jobs. Some progressive managers saw a need for other skills and I got my chance as a landscape architect. At first it was difficult, as people in the organization felt these skills were not needed. Over time as other specialists were hired, such as wildlife biologists and hydrologists, these attitudes changed. For many years, positions in management were still reserved for foresters. I was lucky enough to be one of the few at that time who had the opportunity to become a manager. Over my years with the Forest Service, my life and career opportunities kept changing direction, virtually all unplanned.

As a boy from Iowa, I moved to the West and fell in love with the mountains. In college, I learned skills I never dreamed I could master—then found I could. I moved and changed jobs fourteen times. Many of those jobs were totally different than my college education. It was like starting over with unfamiliar places and people. I moved so often that I left behind many wonderful experiences and friends. Reliving these memories is one reason for this memoir.

I was fortunate enough to meet a wonderful person in my wife, Gretchen Gantert. It was a difficult life for her. She was from Dubuque, Iowa, but had become a big city girl when we met in Denver, Colorado. She had a great job as a school teacher that she had to leave when we moved to the mountains in Dillon, Colorado. We then moved four separate times in eight years, finally ending up in, Milwaukee, Wisconsin, where our children Heidi and Andrew started school and where we stayed for six years. Our last move was to Missoula, Montana, where years ago I had started this adventure as a smokejumper.

How did I come to writing my memoirs? I once read a quote that said, "Being a father is an adventure that takes your heart to places it never had gone before." I shared with my children a letter I had written on an accident I was involved in, and then we talked about other experiences. They encouraged me to write a book about my life story.

Remembering your past is not easy. Things are never exactly how you thought they were. As a result, it's a challenge to delve into not only your history but the history of the organization you worked for throughout your career. It's been an interesting journey.

Why did I name my book *Saving Trappers Lake*? Trappers Lake, in Colorado, is a natural wonder and a special place. What happened at the lake was the most historic event of my career. It was because of my planning at the lake, in 1962, that I got acquainted with Arthur Carhart. Arthur and I both graduated from Iowa State University in landscape architecture. He was the first landscape architect to work for the Forest Service and went on to be an outdoor writer and wilderness advocate. Arthur also played a significant role in preserving the wilderness character of Trappers Lake. Chapter 5 tells the whole story of our involvement. I thought it fitting to honor the memory of Arthur Carhart in the title of the book for his effort in saving Trappers Lake.

My experiences and other job opportunities led me to call myself a forest ranger in this book. There is no official position in the Forest Service called a forest ranger; it's a phrase invented by local lore and the media. Forest Service employees usually referred to a forest ranger as being a manager, a district ranger. However, I felt I lived many different roles having had such a wide and varied career.

Contact the author at: hagie57@gmail.com.

CHAPTER 1

IN THE FOOTSTEPS OF TOM SAWYER

My first successful hunt, about age ten

I WAS A TERRIBLE STUDENT. All I wanted to do was be outdoors. My report cards were all the same. "Jimmy is a bright boy but doesn't apply himself. I should hold him back but I'm going to pass him and hope he improves." They should have held me back. My parents sent me to school when I was four years old. I was small and immature. My parents did very little to get me to study. Why I don't know, as my mother had expectations that I would someday go to college.

My father had to work six long days a week, as did my mother. Church was a big part of our lives: Sunday school, services, dinners, confirmation classes, summer camps, and eventually the choir. The only trips we took were to visit my uncles' farms or to Hannibal, Missouri, to visit other relatives. It was there that I learned about Tom Sawyer and Huckleberry Finn and became engrossed in the stories and adventures.

I was ten years old when my grandmother died. My sisters, Miriam and Leah, had left the house and had started college. Now I was on my own. I spent most of my time hiking the bluffs and along the river bottom of the mighty Mississippi River. Experiences in my youth strongly influenced my free spirit and choice of a profession.

I was born in Burlington, Iowa, on Thanksgiving Day in 1937. Burlington is in the southeast corner of the state and sits on the banks of the river. From the river rise tall limestone bluffs. On top of the bluffs are where most of the homes are located. Down along the river is where the factories and stores were built. In those days, the river would normally flood every spring, sometimes into the town. The town had manufacturing but was probably best known for the Chicago, Burlington and Quincy Railroad corporate headquarters. The C, B & Q employees had a marked effect on the character of the town. Most notably they commissioned Fredrick Law Olmsted Sr., the most famous landscape architect of his time, to design and build Crapo Park on the edge of the bluffs with the same concepts he used in building Central Park in New York City. This setting and the nature of the country had a marked effect on my love and understanding of nature.

My dad's barber shop was the hangout for the local hunters and fishermen. I spent a lot of time listening to their stories. It perked my interest. My dad couldn't take me hunting or fishing so I started to teach myself. I learned how to trap rabbits with a box trap, rode my bike to the woods in the dark squirrel hunting, picked wild asparagus and mushrooms, and fished. In the spring I would spear bullfrogs and gars, a type of primitive-looking fish, in the flood waters of the river. One day I saw this strange bird along the Mississippi. It looked like a very big woodpecker and had a large ivory-colored beak. It wasn't until years later that I saw a picture of an extinct ivory-billed woodpecker. The one I saw may have been one of the last of its breed.

My mother came from a large family of farmers. She had five sisters and five brothers. Aunt Lena was the only sister that I can remember, as the rest died from cancer at a young age. Lena's husband, Uncle Raymond, loved to fish and sometimes hunt. He started taking me fishing and shooting pigeons. I was not very good but was eager to learn. My dad would take a short break once a year to go to my uncles' farms to hunt pheasants. That was the highlight of my year. I couldn't carry a gun but would walk along with the grownups with my BB gun. I was so excited I couldn't sleep a wink.

It was about this time that my parents started to ship me off to my uncles' farms in the summer. I think it was because they both worked, and they needed someone to look after me. I first went to Uncle Walter's. He had a daughter my age, so I would have someone to play with. I dreamed up a game where we would swing across the barn on a rope. Fun! I noticed a rope hanging just outside the open barn door and thought it would be fun to sail out from the barn over the pig pen. About that time my uncle was working in the field and looked up to see this missile flying out the barn door. The rope was attached to a pulley. I landed among the pigs and couldn't get up. After a couple of hour's drive to my hometown, I was in the hospital with a broken ankle. I was never invited back to Walter's place again.

Off to Uncle Sam's farm. Sam was the most successful of the brothers. He had a beautiful farm, house and sharp wife, Aunt Leona. This was Sam's second marriage and they only had one child, a son, Wesley. Wes was a couple years older than me and a brat. I survived a couple of days with him bullying me. My complaints went nowhere. One day he shot me with a BB gun. The shot imbedded in my leg and bled. Leona cut out the BB and patched me up but didn't say a word to Wes. I was mad. He had a toy pistol that I found. He was chasing me around the outside of the house. I stopped behind some bushes and as he approached, I caught him right between the eyes with the pistol butt. Down he went. Fair play, right? Leona didn't think so. Off I went to the next uncle's, my mother's favorite, Uncle Arnold.

Arnold believed in slave labor. He never sent me home, though he had cause, but kept me working. My pay was all the food I could eat, going swimming in town once a month and putting up with his two daughters.

I did get into my share of mischief. Like the time two nephews visited and I organized a roundup. Uncle Arnold raised pigs and had some young ones around thirty pounds each. I thought it would be fun to lasso the pigs and put them in the barn. We spent the day catching pigs. My problem was I didn't let them out. Arnold got home late and discovered the pigs in the barn. He was fuming and came into the house yelling for us to come downstairs. Suspecting what was coming I slipped on a bathing suit under my pants. He had his razor strap out and gave us each several lashes. The other kids were bawling, and I pretended to. At least well enough that he didn't hit me again. I sort of figured he knew.

I spent several summers on his farm and learned a lot about farming. How to drive a tractor and truck, how to use tools, and how to do other farm jobs. I stacked hay bales, sorted livestock, and ran down and killed the Sunday chicken. At about fourteen I refused to go back.

On my own

By now my best friend was Darryl Smyth. I met Darryl at Sunday school. He went to a different school than me but we both loved the out of doors and started tromping the woods together. We had a lot of adventures, but a couple were a bit over the top.

Close to our house was a chicken factory. The building was three stories high. The first story processed the chickens and the top floors are where they were caged. When chickens were delivered to the plant they occasionally escaped. We got the job of catching the escapees. They paid us five cents a chicken for a safe return. Most days none escaped.

We decided to increase our wages. We slipped into the factory and up to the third floor, where we took chickens out of their cages and threw them out the window. I don't know what we were thinking, as chickens can't fly. It wasn't a pretty sight, squawking chickens plunging to the earth with a thud. That was our last day on that job.

Our next big adventure took us to the Mississippi River. It was about a mile from our home. We spent a lot of days just poking around since we didn't have a boat. One day we came upon a fourteen-foot boat in very poor condition outside a bar. This bar sat right next to the river and was elevated in the air on poles to avoid the spring floods. We went to the bar and found the owner, a woman. She said her name was Joe and the boat was hers. She was a huge gal with just a T-shirt on, and nothing underneath. We asked if we could buy the boat. She said, "No. However, if you work for me I will give you the boat." The job was to come down every Monday and clean up the mess from the weekend. We accepted.

What a mess Mondays were. Beer bottles everywhere and all kinds of other trash. It was then we discovered the bar was also a house of ill repute, a whorehouse. It didn't seem to bother us, and we worked on that boat in all our spare time. Over a span of several weeks we really got to like Joe. She would make us sandwiches, give us sodas and advice, and tools to fix the boat. One day as we were working one of Joe's girls came out on the deck opened her wrap and said, "You boys want some of this?" Joe heard her, came out of the bar, and hit her in the mouth. The gal went down, and Joe said, "Don't ever do that to my boys." We soon left Joe's and started a fishing business.

We were now two kids with a fourteen-foot jon boat rowing around the mighty Mississippi. The boat had a square front and flat bottom with two oarlocks. We could really make it move. We had been watching the local commercial fishermen and picked up the basics. We couldn't afford all their equipment, but we started out with a trout line. It consisted of a line with about one hundred hooks spaced one foot apart. We would drop a heavy weight on both ends and a milk bottle float on one end. We didn't burn it up but finally started to catch a few catfish. That was our money fish. We could go door to door and sell them. Our problem was a steady supply.

One day in the early spring we rowed out to a large island to explore. We found a fish basket that must have floated to shore. Fish baskets were used to catch catfish. They were about seven feet long and a foot square. We decided to drag it over to our boat, but to do so we needed to cross a frozen lake on the island. I was in front pulling the basket and Darryl was behind pushing. We were about twenty feet from shore when I fell though the ice into about ten feet of water. I went straight to the bottom and pushed myself up with all my might. As I came out of the water Darryl had shoved the basket up to the hole, so I could grab it and hold on. He swung around and got to shore and then pulled me in. Life saved, but just barely. It was now late afternoon and getting colder, and I was soaking wet. We still had miles to go. Fortunately, Darryl had matches. We built a big fire and roasted my clothes like hot dogs. By dark the clothes were dry enough to put on, but a bit holey. We finally made it home.

Our river adventures went on for a couple of years. Our confidence in ourselves and our ability to survive was growing. During this time, we also took up trapping and predator hunting. We thought we could make money on the furs and the bounty money the county paid for killing what they called "predators." We did the predator hunting together but the trapping, separately. I had a trap line along the Mississippi, mainly trapping muskrats and mink. Occasionally I would get a fox, which paid a good bounty. I would also get racoons, skunks, and sometimes feral cats. They were all tough to deal with. I made money on the muskrat fur, but the price took a dive. I gave up trapping but not before I had the scare of my short life.

I was walking along the river shoreline when I saw a flock of Canvasback Ducks. I couldn't resist and shot one. It fell on the ice on the river. I started out on the ice and as I approached the duck the ice started to crack all around me. I dropped to my stomach and slowly worked my way back to shore. I knew if I fell though it was all over. The current would carry me downstream and under the ice.

One of my first paying jobs was in a shoe store downtown. My mother got me the job. They wanted to make me into a salesperson. I hated it and didn't last long. My next job was at the local pool selling hot dogs and soda. In my spare time I played club baseball and tennis and caddied for members of the golf club. I had friends whose parents belonged to the club. The club had clay tennis courts, top of the line. I played both baseball and tennis with all my spare time and got to be pretty good, especially at tennis.

Until now I had been small, but during high school I grew to my adult size. Since I played a lot of sports, my friends started asking me to go out for high school football. I played flag football with a lot of the guys on the team and was fast and fearless.

I went out during my senior year. It was fun. I became a running and defensive back. Really, I was just learning the game. I didn't play much as we had a great team and eventually won the Iowa state title. About halfway through the season, I got my chance and went out for a pass, caught the ball, and raced down the field. I got hit hard and couldn't get up. No broken ankle but a bad sprain. That ended my football season and probably led to my constant ankle problems. The rest of the school year I spent at the YMCA swimming and playing all the other sports they had, paddleball, handball, and ping pong.

I was now close to graduating from high school and still not doing great in school. I signed up for a mechanical drawing course. Mr. Lucas was my instructor and he really helped me. I discovered I could visualize objects and draw them. In fact, I did it well enough that I got my first A in school. I always wanted to take art but because my grades were so bad I had to take classes like typing. Now I started to learn the basics. That discovery would later influence my education in college.

A New Learning Experience

I graduated from high school and I was headed to college. But first I and another boy from my church volunteered to spend the summer working in a youth center somewhere in the States. This became a real adventure and broadened my education.

We traveled to Pottstown, Pennsylvania by train, farther than I had ever gone. There were kids from all over the country and we had a week of training and evaluation. When they handed out the assignments it became obvious my friend and I were the last on the list. Most kids were divided into groups of three or four and were sent to urban locations. Four girls and four boys including me were being sent to Shannondale Community Center in southern Missouri. I lucked out. It was my cup of tea.

Shannondale was a small community church located on a three-thousand-acre forest preserve thirty miles from Salem, Missouri, the nearest community. The mission of the church was to provide church service to the hill people, but more importantly to provide farming demonstrations of how these people might be able to make a living on their rocky, marginal farms. I came from Iowa with wonderful farmland and generally well-off people. These people were poor, so poor that they struggled to have enough food or clothes. What I learned on my Uncle

Arnold's farm really helped me contribute to this mission.

We roughed it. The boys slept in the upstairs of an old goat barn with no windows, but the barn was open at both ends. We got up at dawn and all chipped in to make breakfast before heading to the fields to plant crops, weed and eventually harvest. By noon it was too hot to work, so we took off to the Current River to swim. Then in the evening we would have services or activities for families and their kids. That was the hardest part. The hill people were very suspicious of us. At first, we would only have a few kids attend our activities.

Our summer home, the goat barn

What really broke the ice was our effort to go out to farms and help them with their chores, from chopping wood to—most of all—putting up their hay. This wasn't like Iowa: no machines. They cut and raked the hay with horses. The hay wagon would move through the field and we would pitch the hay on with pitchforks. When it was full, we would stack the hay in loose stacks for the winter. The hill people did not have many live-stock: a milk cow, maybe a steer or two, and most often a few pigs and chickens. The farmers gave us lunch, which was really depressing. They would give us the best food they had, which wasn't much. We got to the point where we would only take a small portion so they might have food left for themselves.

Our efforts started to pay off. Through word of mouth we gained the hill people's trust and the kids started to come to evening sessions. We soon had over thirty kids. Some of these kids had any number of ailments. There was little or no health care for them. I remember one little boy that looked like he was starving to death. It turns out he was, and he died shortly after we all left to go home.

The preacher who ran Shannondale, Reverend Bucker, was a dedicated man. He and his wife had spent their lives trying to help these people. He did it with very little money or support from our churches. He had a small number of support vehi-cles—a large truck, an old army jeep without a top and a small pickup. Both the truck and jeep had brake problems. I learned the hard way.

We were coming back from our daily swim in the jeep. I was driving and had three passengers, no seat belts in those days. I was coming down a steep hill when the brakes went out. I downshifted but picked up speed anyway. Going through a sharp curve the jeep tipped and I lost one kid. Then I made the next curve and almost crashed into the borrow ditch. As luck would have it, at the bottom of the hill was a stream crossing the road. When I hit that, I bucked another passenger out and into the water. When the jeep came to a halt, I realized what had happened to my friends. My one remaining passenger ended up with a bad cut on his arm. Fortunately, no one was seriously hurt.

The next accident was with the large truck. The whole crew was spending our Sunday getting a load of hay. We were all on top of the hay as the truck approached an intersection with the highway. The brakes went out and the truck started to tip over but the load of hay, with all of us on board, slid off the truck onto the highway. This time it was my turn. I landed flat on my back on the highway. Everyone else was all right. I hurt badly and could hardly move. They thought I might have broken my back. They raced me into Salem but couldn't find a doctor. I suffered a lot that night and woke up in the morning hardly able to move.

However, my desire overcame my judgment. I had been asked to help a couple farmers round up their cattle out in the woods. I had learned how to handle a horse while on my Uncle Arnold's farm. This was the day. I said I was OK—a lie—and off I went to ride all day long. I was very lucky. A day on horseback loosened my back up and I went on to be all right.

The summer was not all work. Reverend Bucker took us all into St. Louis riding in the back of his truck to see a couple of outdoor concerts. We saw *Carousel* and *South Pacific* with the original casts. While there, we stayed in the youth center I could have gone to in the program. Very depressing. Not a good neighborhood. The doors even had to be unlocked for both entering and leaving the building.

It was a very good summer. I had a lot of different experiences, especially a new appreciation for the lives of the less fortunate. I was looking forward to the next step in life, college.

CHAPTER 2

CREATING A PURPOSE

West to Wyoming
Wayne Gieselman, left, Darrel Scarff, right. A scenic stop on our way there.

IN THE FALL OF 1955, I was seventeen and starting my college career at Burlington Junior College, a two-year school that was housed in the same building as my high school. My mom had made it clear I was going to college and was determined that I would go to Iowa State University. My Uncle Arnold was the only one of our relatives who had graduated from college, and he went to ISU.

To get into ISU I had to raise my grade point. I focused on classes I knew some things about, such as government, and classes noted for failing people out of ISU, like English. I had improved in school but still was not very good.

My friend, Darryl Smyth, also went to BJC, and we took up our fishing and hunting adventures again. Darryl had kept up the commercial fishing and now had a nice metal boat, with a motor. I went out fishing with Darryl but found I didn't have the time with my school work. Also, some of my other friends had been after me to go out for the football team. I was reluctant after my ankle injury the year before. I talked to the coach and he convinced me to give it a try.

I spent a few days at practice before the second game. I told my Dad he should come see the team and I would be sitting on the bench. During the game, we punted to the other team and the coach told me to go in on special teams. I tore down the field on the punt and hit the guy catching the ball so hard he flipped over backwards and fumbled the football. My Dad never saw the play. We went on to win the game, and I started as a defensive and running back the rest of the season.

Spring came, and I went out for the baseball team. Another friend said I should try out for the tennis team as they were shorthanded. Not many kids played tennis back then. I got on both teams. Normally they play their games on the same day. I spent a lot of time scheduling my tennis matches. Obviously, this all took time away from my classes, but I had a lot of fun. Now time was creeping along, and I needed to think about my future profession and what I was going to take at ISU.

One day my parents had a man from our church do some landscaping in our front yard. His son and I were high school classmates and we talked about the college he was going to. He asked me what I was going to take in college; I said I wasn't sure, maybe forestry. He asked me what I liked to do, and I said I liked to draw and loved the outdoors. He then told me about a short course he attended at ISU on landscape architecture. In his mind it included dealing with architectural design in an outdoor setting and required skill in drawing.

After that discussion, I went up to Ames, Iowa, where ISU was located and attended their spring fling called Veshia. While there, I toured the landscape architecture department and looked at the projects being displayed. I loved it but thought there was no way I could do that. I signed up anyway.

It's sort of ironic how this all came about. Later in life, I found myself walking the land of some of the best landscape architects and naturists of their time. The first was Aldo Leopold—not a landscape architect but a famous outdoorsman who used to work for the Forest Service. Aldo was from my hometown. His father's factory was not far from my home. Stories had Aldo exploring the same bluffs along the Mississippi River that I roamed.

Then there was Crapo Park, designed by Frederick Law Olmsted Sr. It was one of my favorite places. The park had lots of open space, vistas and hidden treasures.

I didn't put this together until I learned about these men in my classes at Iowa State. Also, I learned about Arthur Carhart and his efforts in saving the Boundary Waters Canoe Area in Minnesota. Arthur was also from Iowa and the first landscape architect to graduate from ISU.

About this time, a Forest Service employee came to our junior college. He was looking for anyone who was interested in a summer job in Wyoming's Medicine Bow National Forest and was at least eighteen years old. I had turned eighteen on November 26, 1955. About twenty-five of us attended his session, listened to his proposal, and signed up to work starting in June. Now I had a job for the summer.

Easter was approaching and the weather was still chilly and windy. My friend, Darryl Smyth, was getting his gear ready to start fishing again. He asked for my help on Palm Sunday. I told him I couldn't because I had to go to church with my parents. Palm Sunday evening I got a call from Darryl's mother. She wanted to know if I had seen him or gone fishing with him. I told her I had not. The next morning at class I was called to the main office, where they told me Darryl had drowned. They found his boat overturned and his body floating nearby. I was devastated. Maybe If I had gone with him it wouldn't have happened. Darryl couldn't swim but always wore a life preserver. They later told me he had hit a sunken stump and I knew how and why it happened. The portion of the Mississippi where he fished had been flooded by a wing dam. Many of the islands were now underwater; the trees had been cut down and removed, but the stumps remained. If Darryl had wandered off course and gone over an island traveling at a high speed it was an accident ready to happen. Had I been with him I could have also died, especially in the cold springtime water. We celebrated Darryl's life and he was buried on Easter Sunday.

West to Wyoming

I finished my first year in junior college and went off to Wyoming for the summer. There is no experience in America like driving out West from the Midwest, particularly in June. As you leave Iowa and start crossing Nebraska the air starts to dry out and becomes clearer. Driving along the Platte River with your windows open, the fresh smell of newly cut alfalfa engulfs the car. As you enter Colorado or Wyoming, off in the distance the mountains suddenly appear. Every year as I left college for my summer jobs I looked forward to the experience. I dreamed that someday I would be able to live out West.

My friend, Wayne Gieselman, drove Darrel Scarff and me in his car. We first went to Rocky Mountain National Park in Colorado then north to Laramie, Wyoming, over the pass on the Snowy Range and down into the Medicine Bow National Forest. We ended up at a small Forest Service ranger station on the west side of the pass. We were about twenty-five miles from both Encampment and Saratoga, Wyoming, in the middle of a lodgepole pine forest with sagebrush-covered meadows.

Our home for the next three months was an old ski hut about a mile from the station. We had electricity and an outhouse, but no running water except a creek flowing next to our building. We walked down the highway in the morning for breakfast at the chow hall, then packed our lunch and started work at 7:30.

Our education started that first morning. Gordon Brown was the district ranger and had spent many years on this district. He was tough and seasoned. He first asked, "Who can use an axe?" I raised my hand along with a few others out of thirty young men. He separated my group from the others and we all went to work cutting trees and bucking them up under his watchful eyes. At the end of the day he picked four of us and we became a separate crew under one of his returning employees. We became the do-everything crew and the rest were on the brush piling crew under a foreman. I lucked out.

We got to do everything. We walked miles of fence and repaired breaks or put in new posts. We dug holes for outhouses, painted buildings, and built a corral. Unfortunately, after the money ran out for those projects we also got to pile brush like the other poor guys, but on our terms. No straw boss, just five guys having fun and building tremendous piles of brush.

Of course, we all were supposed to be a fire crew. We would have training on how to build a fire line and put out fires using nothing but dirt. Very seldom did our district have fires. It was at about 8,500 feet elevation and a bit cool. One day we had a fire call but by the time we got there it was out. We spent the night looking for hot spots. That was the end of our fire season.

Iowa State University

When I returned home, Darryl's parents came by our house. They had started a scholarship fund at Burlington Junior College and wanted to give the first scholarship to me. I was honored. I had been giving some thought about going back to BJC for my second year in college to play football. My mother spoke up and thanked them but said I was going to Iowa State University starting in two weeks. I hadn't even registered.

My mother got on the phone and called the university. Yes, they had room for me in the school but no place for me to stay. She then called a friend whose son was in the Theta Chi fraternity. They said I could stay at their fraternity until I pledged. Off I went to ISU. I ended up pledging Theta Chi and they gave me a board job waiting tables and working in the kitchen. It paid for my food.

I started going to Frisbee House, a youth center run by my church, The United Church of Christ. They had a Sunday get together with an evening meal. I got to know the director, Dr. Jane Molden. She was a very intelligent lady, great athlete and the first person of African heritage I got to know well. We got along, and she invited me to help with the local church youth program.

I was struggling in school and ended up failing my algebra course. It was at eight in the morning and a large class. I also did poorly in other classes and finished that first quarter with a 1.5 grade point average. My second quarter wasn't much better, and I was below a 2.0. One more quarter like that and I would have been out of Iowa State.

One day Dr. Molden asked me if I would be interested in moving into Frisbee House. She had room for four students and one had left. The room required doing house and yard chores. The cost to me would be twenty-five dollars a quarter and all the leftovers from the Sunday meal. What a deal. I was pretty much putting myself though college and this would be an immense help. When I told the frat house I was moving out they told me there was no way I was going to meet my grades without their help. Fortunately, I had two new roommates at Frisbee House that were working on their doctorates who helped me.

I was now into classes that were easier for me, but I still faced algebra again. I was determined to do better. On the first day, I marched into class early and sat in front of the teacher. She had a reputation for being tough but a good teacher. I didn't miss a day and began to understand the math. I ended up erasing my F and helping my grade point. My grade point went above 2.0 and I was out of trouble.

That summer I was accepted into the Forest Service smoke-jumper program in Missoula, Montana. It was a great summer and changed my life forever. More on those experiences later.

My junior year in college was again hard but I liked it. In my landscape architecture classes I had two primary instructors. One was more of an engineer and wanted our designs to be very functional and exact. My other instructor, Professor Hanson, believed in being creative, saying function would come after you start making a living. I learned from both, but my grades were much better under my creative instructor. He taught me how to do old-fashioned renderings using a wash technique, like the old masters. He also gave me a job helping with the local work he did on the side.

I still was living in Frisbee House and active in the youth activities. I had a job at the local church helping with church youth programs. I now had time for a few electives and decided to take a sociology course. One of the sociology professors went to our church and he talked me into taking rural sociology, which was about understanding communities and how they formed and functioned. This class really helped me in later life working in small communities with the Forest Service and learning people's values and networks. He also asked me to help him with the church services he gave to local country churches. I did a lot of the readings and he gave the sermon. He even let me do a couple of sermons, which was scary but a good learning experience.

That fall Frisbee House had an intercollegiate meeting of my church at a camp retreat. All the colleges in Iowa attended. One of the actions they took was to elect a new president. My name—over my objections—was submitted as a candidate. I won. I had no idea what I would do or how to do it. It posed problems for me. I needed to visit every campus but didn't have a car. My dad came to the rescue and bought me a used Studebaker. The other big issue was that I had to give a speech to the statewide ministers' conference, both for the Congregational and Evangelical–Reformed churches. I had never given a speech to that many people in my life, let alone ministers. I first went to the Congregational meeting. The fellow I replaced got up first and gave a great speech. When it was my turn, I froze. I could hardy say my name. I was very embarrassed.

I told Dr. Molden about my experience and she said she would coach me. I wrote the next speech, with her help, and she rehearsed me. I went to the next meeting and felt prepared. I was excited because the minister from my home church in Burlington, Reverend Beck, would be there. As I went up on the stage he got up and left. I gave my speech and it went well, but I was disappointed that Reverend Beck wasn't present. I never forgot the experience and always prepared for my talks in the future.

During the spring quarter the juniors and seniors in my curriculum went on a two-week trip to visit several cities— Milwaukee, Chicago, and Detroit. We visited all kinds of sites and offices associated with our profession. Up until now my class was still working toward a degree in either landscape architecture or urban planning. This trip was supposed to influence which direction we went in our final year. After listening to city planners moan about how little they accomplished with all the politics, I picked the LA (landscape architecture) option. In thinking back, I ended up using my planning education as much as landscape architecture during my career.

That next spring, in 1958, I returned to Missoula, Montana for another summer of smokejumping. I liked the work and guys

I jumped with and needed the money to complete my education. It was exciting and left me with a tremendous sense of accomplishment. Unfortunately, the summer didn't go as planned, as there were very few fires. I left the jumping program with the idea I would return the next year.

When I returned to school, the head of the landscape architecture department called me into his office. He said I was required to have six months of practical experience to be able to graduate. He told me he would give me three months for my "running around" but I needed to get experience in my field during my last summer break. I had hoped to return to smoke-jumping, but my parents were counting on me to graduate. I applied to the National Park Service and a couple of jobs in the Forest Service in Glenwood Springs, Colorado, and Grangeville, Idaho.

I was accepted for both the Glenwood Springs and Grangeville jobs. Having jumped on fires in Idaho, I knew what Grangeville was like. It was a small farming community with the next largest town over one hundred miles away. Not a good choice to increase my landscape architecture skills. On the other hand, Glenwood Springs was a tourist town west of Denver and forty miles from Aspen a famous ski town. I chose Glenwood Springs.

West to Colorado

My job was as a crew leader with a five-person crew. In 1958, Congress created the Outdoor Recreation Resources Review Commission. Its job was to inventory overall recreation opportunities in the country. My job was to inventory possible recreation opportunities throughout the White River National Forest. That included writing reports on all possible opportunities for camping and picnicking as well as exploring and writing reports on unique features, such as caves. It was a job made in heaven for me. From Monday through Friday we would jeep, horseback ride, hike, and of course drive to every site on the forest. The White River is one of the most beautiful and diverse National Forests in the system. It has several Primitive Areas, major rivers such as the Colorado, Roaring Fork, Fryingpan, Eagle, and White and many high-country lakes, with Trappers Lake being one of the largest natural lakes in Colorado. It also has one of the largest ski complexes in North America.

I always wondered why my boss Charles "Chuck" McConnell, the recreation forester, chose me as his crew leader. I was a landscape architecture student. All of my crew were forestry students. At that time only a few landscape architects existed in the Forest Service and they were at the regional level. Most people in the organization didn't know a thing about the profession. As time went by Chuck and I became close friends. I asked him, "Why me?" "Because," he said "You had been a smokejumper. I knew what kind of a person was able to get and do that job. That's the kind of person I wanted."

Years later I better understood what Chuck had meant by this statement. It wasn't about being a smokejumper but being used to hard physical work and performing a difficult and challenging job. Later in life, when I hired someone, I was just as interested in how they developed as a person as I was in their advanced education degree.

I was now twenty-one years old, and the summer of 1959 was filled with adventure: backpacking into wilderness areas, exploring and mapping caves, running wild rivers and enjoying the wonderful entertainment in Aspen. In 1959, there were several young entertainers there, the Limeliters, the Kingston Trio, and others as well. It was quite an education for a boy from Iowa.

My job entailed scheduling our weekly visits to different districts on the forest. We usually split the crew up depending on the type of inventory we were doing. If it was a backcountry trip I usually only had two people go. We had two old army jeeps assigned to my crew. No seat belts or roll bars. A bit dangerous but fun to drive on the steep roads. I then had to schedule where the crew would stay—camp out, or in a Forest Service bunk house or a resort.

By now I was hooked on the Forest Service. I liked the people, loved the country I had worked in, and thought I could

contribute to the mission. I was interested in trying to get a job with them but thought I would have to go back to school in forestry to be hired.

Back at school I reviewed my class schedule and made some major shifts. Since it was my fifth year I had time for several electives. I went to the head of the forestry school and introduced myself and told him I would like to get a dual major in both landscape architecture and forestry. He reviewed my classes and said most would apply to forestry, but I would be faced with at least another year taking timber management classes. As it turned out that wasn't an option as my draft board would turn me down for a one-year extension.

I also looked at my landscape architecture classes. One class was required but I had no use for it. The class was given by a botanist and it was on roses. I went to the head of our department and proposed that I drop that course and substitute a class that I would construct on resort and campground design, which I thought would help me pursue a possible job with the Forest Service. He turned me down, but Professor Hanson, came to my rescue and said the rose class would be a waste of my time and my future job had promise with the course I proposed. Professor Hanson prevailed.

It was fun constructing my own class. I went from master planning to road design, campground design and construction specifications. Professor Hanson was a great help. He preached the philosophy that Frederick Law Olmsted, Sr., relished in his park designs: "It is not the facility that is the focus of your design, it is the relationship of the facilities to their natural setting. Before starting your design, you need to understand the natural condition of the land, identify the special places, the vistas and suitable locations for development." This concept stayed with me during my years as a landscape architect and a planner.

During this time, I had moved out of Frisbee House and joined forces with three other guys to rent a three-story house. Two of them were graduate students in horticulture and then another LA and me. We sublet the upstairs and most of the downstairs to other students. Our goal was to see how cheaply we could live. We came up with a lot of ideas. Some worked, and some didn't. The guys in horticulture had access to the farm products in their fields so we got a ton of potatoes and other crops. One guy was from a farm and brought us a pig, which we had slaughtered. I went to my Uncle Arnold's farm and would help him combine corn. In exchange he would give me chickens and eggs.

We had a recreation room in the basement. Ames, Iowa was a dry town, so we would go to Des Moines and buy cheap beer by the case and then stock our room with it and sell beer on weekends to other students. The word got out and we made a bundle of money, but we were always looking over our shoulder for the law.

Our one loser was pumpkin pies. The horticulture grads got all these pumpkins from the university farm, so we thought we would make a bunch of pies and sell them. One of my roommates had a girlfriend getting her degree in home economics and we asked her for recipes. Making pumpkin pie from scratch is no picnic. We made quite a mess, and when we were done had fifteen pies. They were terrible. Regardless, each of us got by on less than one dollar per day for the year.

When the holidays were approaching, Jane Molden asked me to chaperone a number of students to a massive church gathering in Athens, Ohio. We took a bus from Ames on the long trip to Ohio. While there, the keynote speaker was Martin Luther King Junior. I had never heard of him, but his speech was tremendous. I will never forget it.

My graduation day was special. Both my family and Uncle Arnold's came. After the celebration, my father said to me, "Jim, I will give you anything in the world that I can afford for your successes and graduation." I said, "Dad, I know what I want, and you can afford it. I want you to quit smoking." My Dad was in his mid-fifties and had smoked since he was twelve. He always had a cigarette in his mouth—Lucky Strike. He quit and never smoked again. It had to have added years to his life, as he had a heart condition. He lived to be seventy-eight years old and died in his sleep. The greatest gift of my life.

My dad smoking; I asked him to quit for my graduation present—he did

CHAPTER 3

Photo courtesy of Mike McMillan

Jumping Fires

WHEN I WAS STILL A PLEDGE in the fraternity at Iowa State University, the fraternity had a pledging party for new candidates. I invited a friend who I played football with at Burlington Junior College, Joe Lord. Joe was a year older than me and had worked on the same district in Wyoming as I had worked, but a year before. I asked Joe what he did last summer, and he said he was a smokejumper. "What is a smokejumper?" I asked. He said, "We go to forest fires by parachuting from airplanes." I was fascinated and spent the evening asking him questions. That party changed my life.

It wasn't long before I applied to the Forest Service in Missoula, Montana, for a job as a smokejumper. In late May, I got a letter saying I had been accepted and to report to Missoula in early June. Another fellow from my hometown was also accepted. We rode out together in his car. I didn't know how I got selected, as you were supposed to have 100 hours of fire experience to qualify. I had ten. It turns out my old ranger, Gordon Brown, had added another zero when asked by the base.

I was fortunate to start as a jumper, as I avoided the normal path of what they called a ground pounder, except for my one year in Wyoming. Smokejumpers were supposedly the elite of the Forest Service firefighters. There were over one hundred new recruits when we lined up in front of the loft in June of 1957. I was now nineteen years old. The first week was orientation, first aid, and indoor training. We also did exercises and ran a mile or two every day.

One of the classes was on the 1949 Mann Gulch tragedy, in which thirteen smokejumpers were killed fighting a forest fire. They went over every little detail of how it happened and what they did wrong. It left a lasting impression on me.

You Can't Train Too Much for a Job That Can Kill You

The second week of training was hell. They worked us to a breaking point. In fact, the first day I was so tired that I flopped down on my bunk with my boots on and never got up until morning. We still did our before-breakfast run and then a series of training stations, each designed to strengthen our bodies for a different aspect of smokejumping. We spent a lot of time in our jump suits practicing hooking up inside a plane mock-up and jumping a foot or two to the ground. We then went into the woods and learned how to build a fire line and how to work as a team. The training was intense, and recruits started to drop out. My friend from Burlington quit, as did many others. I was determined to make it. I had never been a quitter. Besides, I had met some great guys. For most of my life I had been sort of a loner and now I had met people who seemed to share my values and who I could relate to.

Finally, we loaded up for our first practice jump. It was an easy jump in an open meadow with our instructors yelling at us though bullhorns as we approached the ground. We were graded on how we handled the chute and our landing. One of my friends, John Wagner, broke his ankle on this first jump and had to leave the program. After seven practice jumps of increasing difficulty, we graduated. I had never been in an airplane. Now I had been in a plane seven times and never landed in one.

Shortly after our last practice jump the new recruits went on the jump list with the "old men." A big lightning storm came though Idaho and ignited a number of fires. Horns blared, and we raced to the loft to see if our name was called. I was on the list, and we suited up and left the base in Missoula, Montana, in a Ford Tri-Motor. The plane held eight jumpers and gear. We were headed for Hells Canyon on the Idaho–Oregon border. It is

Smokejumper Graduates, Missoula, Montana, 1957
The arrow points to me, sitting in the first row of the graduating class.

the deepest canyon in the United States. As we approached the fire we could see smoke rising from a rock outcropping in the middle of the canyon. The spotter dropped a streamer, a long piece of brightly colored cloth or paper, where he thought we might land. We saw it fly past its mark and disappear several thousand feet down. The pilot said, "Way too windy. We're heading back to Missoula."

Soon afterwards we got another fire call. The fire was a new lightning strike in the canyon of the Salmon River, "The River of no Return," in Idaho. Sixteen jumpers took off in our DC-3 and we jumped around mid-morning. We landed on a grass-covered ridge. The fire, named "Pine Creek," was about 1,000 feet below the top of the ridge with the river 2,000 feet farther down—very steep. We slowly worked our way down and started building a line on the east edge of the fire. It was hot and dry with lots of

Missoula's DC-3 Loading Jumpers for a Fire

smoke. By midafternoon we had built a line to the bottom of the fire. At that time four of our crew, including Jim Cherry, a friend of mine and fellow Iowa State student, were sent around to the west side of the fire. The rest of us continued to close our line. We soon ran out of water and Dan Hensley and I volunteered to climb back up to our jump spot and retrieve two five-gallon cans of water. It was now early evening and cooling off. I found my day pack and put on my jacket. I loaded five gallons of water on my back and headed down to our crew. A breeze had come up and the fire started to make runs. The temperature heated up as we got closer to the fire and I was soaking wet from sweat.

The fire was now jumping our line and Jim Cherry and his fellow jumpers were somewhere in the blow up. We yelled as loud as we could but got no answer. We thought they were trapped.

The following quote is from an article Jim Cherry wrote about the fire in a 2003 issue of *Smokejumper*, the magazine of the National Smokejumpers Association.

> Below us the fire began rolling downhill between finger ridges and then making button-hook runs to the top of our ridge, driven by a 25-30 mph wind—each time coming closer and hotter with its oily black smoke. With each run of the fire our line was holding and we were staying ahead of the flames—just barely. The next run would bring the flames right over us. "What are we going to do when that next run comes?" was the question we were shouting with parched throats over the roar of the fire. The response was: "Drop your shovel, keep your Pulaski and head for that talus slide below us."
>
> With another roar the fire started its run upslope towards us and we took off for the slide area, laid down, put our faces in the rocks for fresh air and the fire swept over and around us. We had survived! After waiting for another couple of hours we tried again to make our way back up to the top, past our charred shovels, and spent the night with the rest of our crew, watching the fire gobble up our line. Four of us had cheated death in that blow-up and we knew it.

When Jim and his crew finally made it safely back to join the rest of us I was chilled and had to take off my wet jacket and shirt. I spent the night wrapped in a piece of tarp. We heated some water and I had the first cup of coffee in my life.

The fire was now bigger than we could handle and the next morning two more planes arrived, and the air was filled with multi-colored parachutes. They held sixteen more jumpers from Missoula and eight from the McCall, Idaho, base.

Our crew then had another close call. We were heading across a rock slide when lookouts started yelling "Rock! – Rock! – Rock!" We were in a narrow spot and had virtually no time to run. We dove for cover behind any large rock we could find. I remember rocks the size of basketballs, or larger, flying over my head. Fortunately, no one was hurt. We put the fire out but not before they had dropped a total of forty smokejumpers to fight it.

Finding our way home was an adventure. After a 2,000-foot descent we came to the rapids of the Salmon River. Suddenly a jet boat arrived and shuttled all the jumpers to where the road ended. We slept on the ranger station lawn and then took buses to Salmon, Idaho. From there we flew back to Missoula in our DC–3.

A High Country Two-Man Fire

Every jumper dreams of getting a high-country wilderness two-man fire. I was fortunate to have had several during the two years I jumped. My first was in the Scapegoat Primitive Area north of Lincoln, Montana. Normally these fires were small ones caused by lightning and not difficult to put out. They would normally drop only two jumpers. The exciting part was the wilderness trip to get out. You needed to use your woods skills and sometimes be forced to live off the land. After the fire was out you packed up your jump gear and tools, weighing over 100 pounds, and carried them to a trail or other spot where they could be picked up by a packer or helicopter. Then with only a small pack holding a few clothing items, a fishing line, a head lamp, and what food you still might have, you hiked to where the Forest Service would pick you up. In most cases, you had never been in the country before and had seen it for the first time from a plane.

Over the years, I had learned how to find my way in the wild. Only once did I ever get lost. That was on an island in the middle of the Mississippi River. I had gone into the swamp to shoot ducks and walked for a couple miles when I ended up on the edge of the river. Rather than retrace my steps I decided to take a short cut back to our duck blind. After two hours I ended up at the same spot on the river's edge. I had walked in a circle. I then retraced my original path and made it back at dark. That taught me a lesson I never forgot.

As part of our training I paid close attention on how to read a map and use a compass to navigate in wild country without knowing a thing about where you were, or what lay ahead. That training and practical experience paid off the rest of my life, in the army infantry, with the Forest Service, and in my hunting adventures.

My most exciting two-man fire was in some of the wildest country in the United States, the Bob Marshall Primitive Area, which was designated a Wilderness Area in 1964. The fire was lightning-caused and in an old burn. My partner Stan Norgaard and I spent our allotted time putting the fire out. The last day it flared up and we had to stay longer. Unfortunately, we had run out of food. The only thing we had to eat was huckleberries. For two days that is what we ate, and it didn't sit well with our stomachs.

The best part of this fire was lying under the stars with the northern lights dancing in the sky. I had never seen this kind of display before. They lit up the entire sky. Of all the years I spent overnight in the northern forests, this was the best display I ever saw.

A plane checked on us and we put out a marker indicating it would take us longer to put out the fire. They dropped a note telling us to be at Big Prairie Ranger Station in two days to get picked up by a plane at 8:00 A.M. We had a day to put out the fire and a day and night to get to Big Prairie twenty miles away. The fire took more time than we thought so we had to hump to get to the station.

After dropping our jump gear at a nearby trail for the Forest Service packer, we stopped at a small stream to catch some cutthroat trout for a meal. As we were fishing I came upon a fresh bear track big enough to put my foot in. While we were on the fire we had counted seven different bears feeding on huckleberries. This had to be a big grizzly. We immediately took off down the trail with only a couple of small fish. We came to a wilderness Forest Service cabin at the head of Hahn Creek and broke in. The only thing we could find to eat was pancake mix. We cooked up the fish, finished off the mix and headed down the trail.

It was now late afternoon and we had a way to go. We heard some mules braying and thought they might be in a Forest Service camp. As we approached the camp a guy was ringing a dinner bell and yelling, "Come and get it!" We yelled back, "We'd love to." It was an outfitter with a group of architects from San Francisco. They gave us dinner. It was now dark, and we said we had to go—we had a plane to catch. They were stunned and said you can't go out there at night, but we did.

We walked along in the dark almost in a trance when suddenly this very big animal came running down the trail toward us. We dove off the trail at the same time the animal arrived. Whatever it was, it must have sensed our presence and dove off the other side of the trail into the river. Lots of splashing and then gone. What, we don't know . . . bear, moose, or elk?

We were now to the point where we thought we should be close to the ranger station at Big Prairie. We then came to a trail sign that said, "Ford of the South Fork." We knew that it meant we had to wade the river in the middle of the night. From the sound of the river, below the ford, there was rushing water through the rocks and possibly rapids. We tied our belts together and with the aid of poles slowly crossed the river. After a while we caught the reflection of the moon on tents and walked into the station. The next morning a Ford Tri-Motor landed and took us back to Missoula.

When the season ended, I caught a ride back to Ames and college. There were three of us in the car. We took turns driving, each taking two hours on and four off. At around two in the morning I was riding shotgun and asleep. I woke up to see the car slowly drifting off the highway. As I grabbed for the wheel the driver woke up and jerked it. We immediately rolled over landing on our side in the middle of the highway. No one was hurt but one side of the car was beaten up and the doors jammed. As we were surveying the scene we could see a car coming far off in the distance. Hooray, help! As the car drove up this drunken voice said, "Are you ok?" We said "yes" and he drove off. We now started to rock the car hoping to get it back on its wheels. Suddenly, the car righted itself and proceeded to roll into the borrow ditch. The car owner said, "What do we do?" I said, "I'm going to drive it out." We got in, and I floored it going as fast as I could and then side-hilled up the ditch to the highway. That was a fitting, and lucky, end to my summer.

In the summer of 1958, I returned to my smokejumping job in Missoula after my junior year in college. We took a few practices jumps and then waited for the fire season. Unfortunately for us, it was a wet year. The base sent five of us to the Moose Creek Ranger Station in the Selway Primitive Area in Idaho until the fire season heated up. Moose Creek is 30 miles from a road and is accessed by trail or by air. They have a small airstrip there to support the district and provide access for fire control.

Our job was to help extend the runway by cutting adjacent timber. The district ranger told us we had to use crosscut saws, rather than power saws. We had already heard he was not fond of smokejumpers. We soon found out. He told us every week one of us would have to work in the kitchen helping the cook. We objected but he said if we wouldn't do it he would have us fired. We drew straws and Bob Wilson got the first week and I got the last week. Bob had a miserable week. The cook would sleep in and Bob would have to get up extra early to start the coffee and cook breakfast for all the crews. This went on week after week. Informally we objected to our boss in Missoula, but he was new and didn't want to back our concerns. However, he did tell the district ranger to give us a variety of jobs that would help us in our firefighting mission.

Bucking timber—no OSHA inspectors here

The next week we were sent eleven miles up Moose Creek to maintain trails. We hiked and followed the district packer with all our gear and food. When we arrived at a wilderness cabin we found that the packer had had a confrontation with the district ranger and had decided to quit. He left us with a pack string and a ton of gear and took off down the trail. We worked trail for a couple of days, and then the pack string panicked, taking off for the ranger station when a couple of bears came by. We hiked back to the station and found the district ranger had put all the blame for the situation on us.

He put us back on tree cutting and while cutting a large ponderosa pine with Roger Savage, I managed to cut my leg with our crosscut saw. It was a deep cut and needed to be stitched. Had I been smart, I would have asked to be returned to Missoula but instead I treated the wound myself and wrapped it tight. It healed fine, but I still have the scar.

Later a stack of trees a bulldozer had bunched up caught on fire. No one knew why but it was a hot fire. The ranger directed us to put the fire out and we said only if you give us power saws. The fire was beginning to get away and he agreed to give us the saws. We put the fire out.

It was now after the 4th of July and our summer was flying away. My week of kitchen duty was coming up and I had made up my mind to say no and face the consequences. As the week approached we got the call to return to the smokejumper base. We were happy campers.

On a side note, one day I got a radio call from Missoula. My mother had called them. They piped the call over the radio to me at Moose Creek. She wanted to know if I was OK. It turns out she was watching TV and they showed firefighters getting out of a helicopter and she said, "That's what Jim is doing." Dad said,

The Moose Creek Smokejumpers

Left to right: Roger Savage, Bob Wilson, Charlie Bull, me, and Jim Thompson.

Fighting a fire flare-up

"No, he's jumping out of airplanes." After two summers, she had just figured it out.

The rest of the summer was slow for fires, but I did have a few incidents worth sharing. We had a fire call to go to the Salmon River to jump a grass fire. We flew over in a DC-3 with sixteen jumpers. Usually in a large jump we jumped a three-man stick (or three people at a time). As I left the plane my two partners dropped below me after our chutes opened. The next thing I knew, I was climbing in elevation. The plane I jumped out of was now below me, and I had two airplanes circling my position. I was caught in an updraft going straight up and was now over 2,000 feet above the ground. Then I came straight down and landed without incident.

On another fire on the Salmon they dropped forty-six jumpers from both the Missoula and McCall, Idaho, base. Normally they didn't drop that many jumpers, but they were trying to head the fire off before it got to the wilderness. It was a windy day and the spotter told us to go in backwards. The reason is that our chutes had a forward speed of about six miles per hour. By going backwards, we could reduce our forward speed by that much in a wind. When I came in on the side of the mountain I hit so hard that I did two somersaults. I was fine but several jumpers were injured. I was assigned to medical duty and spent the night treating the injured and giving pain shots. The next morning the injured were airlifted off the mountain.

After the fire was out we all worked our way down to the Salmon River and the road. We had to stay the night for our bus ride home. While waiting, we were lounging on the sand next to the river. A Forest Service official came by and gave us a warning that we shouldn't go in the river because it was dangerous. As if by command about thirty smokejumpers stripped down and dove in the river, bodies bobbing up and down through the rapids. That's what made the job so much fun.

I got a fire call for a fire in Glacier National Park. This was a two-man fire. My partner was Ron Reintsma. We flew up the North Fork of the Flathead River. The fire was on a ridge above Logger Lake and going over the hill. We couldn't jump because of nearby lightning so we left and landed in Kalispell, Montana. When the rain cell passed we again approached the fire and found some rain had knocked down the flames. We jumped and landed in a young stand of lodgepole pines. Nice landing. We hit the fire running trying to get a line on the uphill side before it heated up again. After a couple hours, we felt good about our line and believed we could control the fire.

We usually didn't have radios on our jumps, but the Park Service insisted. I called the park fire officer and told him we had the fire in control and would finish our line and start mopping up. He didn't believe me. He had flown the fire when we first did and saw it blowing up. He had ordered twenty-four men to begin hiking in to help. I insisted we had it and didn't see a need to send more men. It was now Friday, and we lived for weekend fires because we could get overtime with double time. I saw a long weekend ahead and lots of college funds. The fire officer finally said he would send six men to relieve us and we were to hike out the next morning. So much for overtime.

My next fire jump, and one of my last, was another memorable jump. Eight jumpers answered a fire call to go to the Mission Mountain Primitive Area. The fire was above Crystal Lake in very rough country with a series of rock ledges and heavy timber. In fact, when we were circling to find a jump spot the spotter was frustrated and finally picked an area with what he said was "second growth timber." As I approached the ground these supposedly small trees were looming up to 150 feet tall, and our let-down ropes were only 100 feet long. I saw a small opening and steered to a small green spot in the middle. I landed on my seat on what turned out to be a granite rock covered with moss. I sat there for a very long time before I could get up.

There was water close to the fire and we ordered pumps and hose to fight it. Within an hour after setting up the pumps we had flooded the fire and it was out. Now the fun began. The district had told us to take our gear to Crystal Lake. We started to lower a ton of gear cliff after cliff by rope until we got down by dark. The next morning, we called the district and told them we could build a raft and float the gear to the other end of the lake where there was a trail. They agreed. Day two we built a huge raft. The next day we loaded the raft and it sank into the mud. Then we moved the gear down the lake where the water was deeper. We again loaded the gear on the raft and it sank again. It was now Thursday night and we called the district and said we would spend the weekend and build a trail down the lake to the existing trail and they could then bring in a pack string. They responded by telling us to get to Lindberg Lake *now* and we would be picked up by boat and then driven home. Again, so much for weekend overtime.

When we arrived at the base, no one was around. There was a note on the bulletin board inviting everyone at the base to a party at a girls' camp across from Lindberg Lake. It seems a group of these campers had run into some of our fellow jumpers on a project in the Bob Marshall Primitive Area and thought they were nice boys.

We piled into our cars and back up to Lindberg Lake. The "party" consisted of about seventy-five jumpers and twenty girls, most fifteen years of age or under. The lady running the camp was panicked and guarded the door. The jumpers danced with each other and threw dice. It reminded me of *Seven Brides for Seven Brothers*.

I left for school with another jumper and started across Wyoming in my Studebaker. Everything went well until we were out on the plains and a girl passed me. I sped up and passed her, but she again passed me. We were racing down the highway side by side when my car blew up. I limped into Thornton, Wyoming. It was a Sunday, and nothing was open. The next day I junked the car, shipped my gear home, and started to hitchhike.

Hitchhiking is not much fun, especially in the high desert of Wyoming. We got rides with a carnival worker with a loaded gun, a drunk, and a gal in a bathing suit who dropped us off at her ranch road fifteen miles outside of Casper, Wyoming. We finally got a ride with a salesman going to Cheyenne, Wyoming.

We were walking through Cheyenne when the police stopped us. They put us in their car and started downtown. I asked where they were taking us, they said "to jail." When I asked why they said we were vagrants. "What's that?" I asked. "That means you have no money." I pulled out my summer's earnings, about two thousand dollars, and told them that was my money from smokejumping. They were shocked and said we would get robbed in that town. They took us to the bus depot and told us to buy a ticket home. It was now getting dark, so I asked the station clerk where the bus stopped the next day and he said, "Lincoln, Nebraska." We got off the bus in Lincoln and hitchhiked to Ames, Iowa, and school.

During my two summers as a smokejumper I grew from a boy to a man. I learned to cope with adversity and developed the ability to survive under extreme conditions. Jumping out of airplanes into the mountains teaches you the importance of attention to detail. It taught me how to operate with others as a team and to follow orders. Most importantly it gave me the self-confidence to fight for what I believed in.

I was fortunate to become a smokejumper, something I will always cherish. From 1940, when the smokejumper program was started, until just recently there had been only 6,000 smokejumpers. I was one of the lucky few.

Smokejumper Landing
A refresher jump on the runway at Moose Creek, made during a slow fire year.

CHAPTER 4

THE WHITE RIVER NATIONAL FOREST

WILDERNESS, WORLD-CLASS SKIING, WILD RIVERS, AND OUTSTANDING SCENERY

The Maroon Bells near Aspen, Colorado

AFTER MY GRADUATION in 1960 from Iowa State University as a landscape architect, I got a letter from the draft board with a notice to report for the military draft. Chuck McConnell had offered me a job for the summer doing recreation facility design, a fantastic opportunity if I wanted to get a job with the U.S. Forest Service. I went to the draft board office and asked for an extension to work the summer. The clerk said they didn't grant extensions, but I could go before the entire board with my request. I took several of my drawings and my master plan from my senior year class and made my presentation. I started by saying I was not trying to get out of the draft but put myself in a position for a job when I finished my duty. They agreed with me and granted an extension until December of 1960.

I headed back west to Glenwood Springs, Colorado. Chuck had hired an assistant for me, Walt Werner. Walt was a ranch kid from northeast Colorado. He had enlisted in the Navy and was accepted into its flight program. He had gone thought the entire program when his eyesight started to change, and he was let go from the service. Walt was a great guy and we became good friends.

That summer I immediately got called out on a fire. To the west of Glenwood, the National Forest blends with the Bureau of Interior lands, most of which are covered with oak brush, a species that when it burns goes up like gasoline. We got to the fire in midafternoon. We were on the uphill side of the burn and it was quiet. The fire boss wanted us to go down the hill through live oak brush and start a line at the fire's edge. I objected, saying that if we got an afternoon wind we would be trapped and couldn't come back up the steep hillside. He dismissed my concern, but the district ranger had arrived and supported me, saying it would be easier to wait until morning and the loss of the oak brush that might burn was not important. The wind came up and the fire ran to the top of the ridge. All that remained were sticks of blackened wood. We would have died. Years later and one mountain to the east the same thing happened on Storm King Mountain. But in that episode fifteen firefighters needlessly lost their lives.

The Forest Service had received a large budget to improve outdoor recreation opportunities for the public. Chuck had lined up several projects for me. A lot of them were small campgrounds but others were much larger. My field surveying work was much different than what I had learned in college. In college, we were usually given a plat that showed the site and its information. I never had that kind of information until later in my career. I used a table, called a plane table, about twenty inches square with waterproof plastic on top. The table was mounted on a tripod. I had a survey instrument that I could use to determine distance and the difference in elevation from my location to the spot where Walt held a rod. I would first flag out the road locations then the other facility locations, such as camp spots or toilet locations. I would then locate the land features such as tree lines, steep slope areas or natural attributes. It was labor intensive, but when I was done I would have a rough design drawn out on the table. I would then go to the office and draft up my plan.

To start the process, I would go to the site, walk around and tie flags on trees for road centerlines or other features. Often, I would say, "No, this won't work," pull the flags and start over again. Walt would get upset. This went on day after day. We had our differences, but I reminded him I was the pilot, not him.

I can remember one time we were doing a site design above Aspen. We had to wade the Roaring Fork River and I had just pulled a bunch of flags and said we would redo them tomorrow. I was wading the river with my survey equipment when Walt started throwing rocks at me and getting me and my equipment wet. Before long we were in a water fight, no hard feelings just a lot of laughs.

One day my boss Chuck asked me to review a site plan for a campground at Maroon Lake outside of Aspen. Maroon Lake is in a magnificent setting at the foot of the Maroon Bell Peaks that rise to over 14,000 feet. At that time the existing road ran up along the shoreline to the end of the lake. Cars would pull up close to the lake and people would have their picnics right on the shoreline. The ground was worn out and the lakeshore was devoid of vegetation.

The site plan had been drawn by a new landscape architect out of the regional office in Denver. Chuck asked me what I thought of the plan and I said I'd rather hear what the ranger who manages the site thought. Chuck arranged for me to talk to the district ranger, a big Swede by the name of Neil Edstrom.

I met with Neil and he drove me up to the lake. As we arrived there were semi-trucks driving up the alpine meadow next to the lake. Neil was livid. He said the trucks belonged to a group of high-powered people who conducted trail rides every summer, The Roundup Riders of the Rockies. The trucks were bringing in their livestock, food, tents and the bar. He said there was nothing he could do about it. The regional forester condoned it. We spent the day talking about what Neil wanted to see from a management and public use standpoint and he said, "Can you find a way of stopping this kind of resource damage?"

A Road Once Went to the End of Maroon Lake
My recommendation to remove the road was approved.

I drew up a plan that I thought met Neil's goals and the site's capabilities. It was my first major job. The first thing I called for was to eliminate the road from the lakeshore and dead-end it away from the lake. I then designed a new road that went up the mountain side but would be hidden in a grove of aspen trees. Off this road, I designed two parking lots that would allow the day user to hike down to the lake and on into the Maroon Bells–Snowmass Wilderness Area. The lots were not visible from Maroon Lake. Neil liked my plan but said, "I don't think the forest engineer will go for eliminating a road."

Neil was right. Neither the forest engineer Howard Kelso nor Chuck McConnell's boss, the forest lands staff Paul Hauk, approved. We all met at the lake, including Forest Supervisor

Ed Mason. I made my presentation, there was discussion, and Ed turned to Neil and said, "What would your decision be, Neil?" Neil said, "I like the plan." Ed said, "So do I." The road was ripped out and reseeded and the parking lots built. Many years later, most people don't know a road ever existed along the shore of Maroon Lake. Many assume it's in a Wilderness Area.

The Army

The summer went well, and towards August Chuck said they would like to offer me a full-time position with the Forest Service. It was my dream. Chuck knew of my draft status and said he had talked to the local commander of the army reserve unit in Glenwood Springs and he might offer me an alternative. I met with the commander and he said if I joined his unit I would only have to do six months of active service and would be out by next summer. The only catch was that I would have to be in the active army reserves for seven years. I signed up and went into the army on December 1, 1960.

I was assigned to Fort Leonard Wood, Missouri, for basic training. At that time, Leonard Wood was one of the primary recruit (boot camp) training centers in the country. It was an old camp with barracks so old you could see through the sides of the buildings. All the buildings were heated by coal burners. Every morning you woke up with coal tar in your nose and throat. The army does some stupid things. One of which was every morning you fell out with all your clothes and equipment on. We would then march roughly seven miles to the rifle range. By the time we got there we were soaking wet from sweat. Then we would stand around and freeze. They would bring us our lunch, which was frozen. We then marched home. Within a couple of weeks most of the recruits had health problems. I was hanging in there but by a thread. The army decided to give us a two-week break during the holidays. Usually they gave that after boot camp. I got on a train to St. Louis, Missouri, got a room at the YMCA and slept for forty-eight hours. After I got home it took me a week to recover.

At the end of boot camp, they gave us our assignments for further duty. I assumed that being a college graduate, I would get an assignment in a field close to my major. Wrong. I was assigned to an infantry unit and was headed to Fort Dix, New Jersey, for advanced infantry training. I called my commander in Glenwood Springs, and he said that's the way the army works. In hindsight, it was a stroke of luck. I liked the out-of-doors and exercise, and I got a lot of both in the infantry.

Fort Dix turned out to be heaven compared with Fort Leonard Wood. I was fifty miles from New York City and less than that to Philadelphia. The army had lots of perks in both places. I could stay at the YMCAs for little or nothing. My weekends were free, so I would tour the cities. New York was great. For a young man from Iowa, my trips to the city opened a new world. I went to all the museums, hiked all over the park that Frederick Law Olmsted Sr. had designed, Central Park, and took in the other events. I went to all the attractions and enjoyed the socials the Armed Forces provided.

For the most part I did all this on my own, but I did make a friend in my unit who was from New York and Jewish. He invited me to his home for Passover. It was a great experience. His father owned a factory that made fancy lace. Their home was very different. It was three stories high but not wide. Overall it was quite large. In the back, they had an outside patio. While in New York we toured the city and went to Coney Island. I rode my first roller coaster there. The highlight was going to a big Jewish holiday celebration. We went to a penthouse in uptown New York with lots of guests and food, a unique experience for me.

I spent the next seven years in the army reserves and became a drill sergeant. Our mission was to provide basic training to new recruits if we were ever called to active duty. We normally met twice a month and then spent two weeks every year at an army basic training fort. The army was not my favorite job, but I enjoyed the people in my unit. My job entailed giving training presentations to recruits, which required developing lesson plans and presentations. These experiences proved to be helpful in my career with the Forest Service.

The men in my unit were all from the vicinity of Glenwood Springs, Colorado, and from a variety of backgrounds. They were also great contacts in the communities I worked in. Over the years, we became good friends and I enjoyed our summer trips on active duty to many different forts around the country.

One assignment I will never forget. We went to Columbia, South Carolina, to Fort Jackson. When we arrived at the base the platoon sergeants we were assigned to replace for the next two weeks asked our four platoon sergeants, including myself, to go on a disciplinary run with them and some troublemaking recruits. We said sure. When the recruits arrived, we knew we were being conned. They were all athletic young men. What the base sergeants didn't know was our sergeants were outdoor guys and also in great shape. Besides, we had just arrived from Colorado from an elevation of over 5,000 feet. Fort Jackson was at about sea level. Two miles into our run we hadn't even broken a sweat while their T-shirts were soaking wet. We glanced at each other and asked to stop. They thought they had us. We suggested we race the last half-mile back to the base. We left them struggling to keep up. After a couple of beers at the base lounge they told us the last group of reserves from New York City was a disgrace to the army and they cooked up this run to teach the next group a lesson, us. It backfired on them. They let us take over their company and took a little vacation.

In 1967, I was approaching my discharge date from the army reserves when our company got orders to report to full-time duty. It was during the time when the Viet Nam war was heating up. This was in August, just before my discharge date in September. I would have had to go on active duty, and with an infantry background would have probably had to go to Nam. Around the middle of September, they withdrew the order. I almost flew out the door.

My First Full-Time Job

By spring of 1961 I was discharged from active duty in the army and returned to Iowa. Chuck McConnell had been holding my temporary job in Glenwood Springs for me. As I was packing to leave from my parents' home, I couldn't find my favorite white boots that I had had since I started smokejumping. When I asked my mom, she said, "You mean those old beat-up things?" One hundred and fifty-dollar boots down the drain.

When I arrived back in Colorado my summer was filled with design jobs. Walt Werner, having graduated from college with a degree in forestry, had returned to be my assistant.

Early that summer I was called to a fire on the Glenwood District of the White River National Forest. During the night, I fell through a beaver den that was on fire and had a burn on my ankle. I had it treated and two days later had blood poisoning. This time I went to a different doctor and he said it was a third degree burn and would take months to heal. I struggled with it all summer but still had a fire call to go to Montana on a major fire. I thought I could make it, so I went. The fire was on the Clearwater National Forest in Idaho. I was a sector boss and worked the line for a couple days. One evening I was dressing my wound when the fire boss came by. When he saw the wound, he told me I would have to leave. I convinced him I could do other things, and he assigned me to be the air control officer.

There were a couple of injured jumpers on the fire and they told me they were going back to Missoula for a big party on the weekend. I then told the fire boss I should probably see a doctor, so he released me to go to Missoula. What a party! My good friend Bob Wilson poured me onto a plane headed for Denver at the end of the weekend. While on the plane I fell asleep. When I woke up, there was a beautiful girl sitting next to me. She was Miss Wyoming and was heading for the Miss America pageant.

Towards the end of the summer of 1961, Chuck McConnell said my appointment was approved. I was a full-time employee of the White River National Forest and one of the first landscape architects the Forest Service had hired during the modern era. I was twenty-two years old. Having worked on the forest for three summers and been on a number of fires with many different folks, I was well accepted as one of them. I was interested in everything they did and always looked for opportunities to broaden my education. I got on survey crews slope-staking roads; I marked timber for sale; and I went out on range conservation inspections.

Now I had time to get back to the hunting and fishing I so enjoyed. I used to eat at a small diner in Glenwood Springs and one day the owner, Don Kiel, asked me if I knew where there might be some turkeys. I had seen some turkeys on top of the Flat Tops about fifty miles from Glenwood. They were the first turkeys I had ever seen so I had gone to the library to read up on them. I told Don I had, and he asked me if I would guide him and another fellow by the name of Bob Veltus. I agreed.

Bob was about ten years older than me and owned a drive-in restaurant in Glenwood. He was tall, about six feet four inches and a great outdoorsman. We became lifelong friends and he and his wife, Lois, became my parents away from home. They had me over for all the holidays and Bob and I would go hunting every year, even after I moved away.

Bob had a Gordon setter named York, an unbelievable hunting dog. Bob took me up on the Flat Tops hunting blue grouse. I will never forget the experiences we had. The Flat Tops are a mountain plateau rising to over 12,000 feet in elevation. The area is covered by huge meadows with aspen and spruce groves. We would hunt the grouse in the big meadows. People thought we were crazy, but York would find coveys of grouse out in the open. I was so impressed with York that my first bird dog, Shadow, was a Gordon setter I had shipped from back east.

My first fall in Colorado, I did a lot of hunting. I rented a locker and ended up shooting three deer, an elk, mallard ducks, a turkey, and many grouse. Don Campbell was my roommate and all we ate was wild game. We supplemented the meat with wild mushrooms. Don knew a little about mushroom hunting. Basically, all you needed to know is whether they will kill you or not. We got to know about six or seven various kinds and were careful about what we picked and ate.

Winter in Colorado was fast approaching. In fact, that Labor Day a group of my friends and I went spelunking at Fulford Cave outside of Eagle, Colorado. We entered the cave in the early morning and when we returned in the late afternoon the entrance was covered by snow. We dug out of more than a foot of snow. The snow continued all fall, and by Thanksgiving the ski areas in Aspen, forty miles away from Glenwood, were opening early. I was excited.

All my friends were skiers, my roommate Don Campbell, my boss Chuck and his wife Lucy, my friends Neil and Karen Edstrom, and Dick and Janet Serino. I couldn't ski but I was bound and determined to learn. One of the mechanics in our vehicle shop used to run a small ski area by Grand Junction, Colorado. He knew how to fix and maintain Poma lifts, a kind of surface lift that pulled the skier uphill. The owner of Aspen Highlands, Whip Jones, had hired our mechanic to maintain his two Pomas and the mechanic asked if I could be his helper. Whip said he would give me a season pass if I would help. I thought it was a great deal.

I went out and bought old Head skis, number 110, a parka, boots and all the other clothes I needed. Opening day, it snowed a foot of new powder. My friends, took me to the top of the Thunder Bowl at Aspen Highlands, a steep run on the face of the mountain. I took one header after another. I didn't know what I was doing. I was totally exhausted and discouraged. The question going around in the bar after skiing was, "Will Jim ever be a skier?"

I was on a mission. No more skiing with my friends. I would go over to Buttermilk Ski Area across from the Highlands. It was a beginner area where Aspen Ski Corporation would send all their first-time skiers. There was an instructor there who had a good reputation and I looked her up. I could barely afford the lift ticket, so I would stand off to the side and listen to her, then practice along with her students. She would glance my way and give me a dirty look. This went on for a couple of weekends. Finally, she came over looking very upset and I told her I couldn't afford a lesson, but she was supposed to be the best instructor on the mountain. I said I would leave if she said so. She said—like a drill sergeant—"Get in line with the other students." By Christmas my friends called me the fastest snowplow in the West. From then on, I averaged at least sixty days of skiing a year for ten years and after many more lessons ended up an expert.

While in Aspen our gang was a party bunch. Don Campbell and I would head up to Aspen every Friday evening and stay at the ranger station bunkhouse. It wasn't heated, but we didn't care. When we had fresh powder, we would storm the mountain. On the nice days, we would pack a huge lunch with lots of wine and climb out to a point at Aspen Highlands overlooking the valley. Our outings became known, and soon Whip Jones, the owner, his wife, and others started joining us. It became the picnic spot. After we all moved away from Aspen, Whip expanded the area. If you ever go there be sure to ski "Wine Ridge," the run named after our picnics.

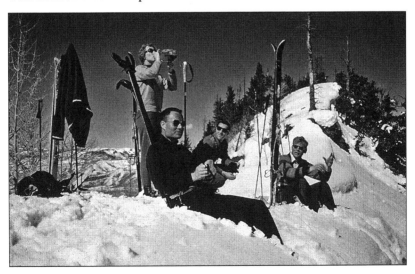

Picnic on wine ridge at Aspen Highlands Ski Area
From left: Karen Edstrom, Chuck McConnel, Dick Serino, and Neil Edstrom.

I was having fun as a Forest Service employee. I was designing recreation sites and facilities, marinas, and all sorts of other jobs, but my smokejumping background kept calling me. I had gained more experience on fires and had worked my way up to a division boss. Most of the fires I went on were fall hunting fires and not all that hot, but they still were interesting. The most interesting was a fire at an army facility, Camp Hale, located just outside of Leadville, Colorado. Camp Hale was the site of the 10th Mountain Division training camp and was run by the army at Fort Carson, Colorado. At that time the post was closed to the public. Guards manned the entrance. They had a forest fire and would not let the Forest Service send in firefighters. They brought in army troops from Fort Carson but needed expertise on how to fight the fire. I was on the overhead team brought in to provide direction.

As we drove into the base I noticed they had training facilities like the ones we had to train smokejumpers back in Missoula, Montana. When we met up with our army officers, I asked one of them, "Are you training people to do low-level mountain jumping?" The next thing I know two guys drove up in an army jeep. They were not army but dressed in black pants and white T-shirts. They said, to me "Get in!" and we drove down to a barracks. They interrogated me, asking how I knew about the training facilities. When I told them I had been a smokejumper, they wanted to know when, where, and who I knew. After two hours, they took me back to the fire and said, "You don't tell anyone anything."

Some things I figured out for myself. I thought they were CIA. I also noticed several very small people walking around. I figured they were Asian but did not know from which country. I did as I was told and put the incident out of my mind until just recently. In the last couple years, the CIA files have been made public and the whole story unveiled. This was a secret base that was started by President Truman and carried on until President Kennedy. The purpose was to train Tibetans in mountain warfare to counter the Chinese invasion of Tibet. This included training in low-level parachute jumping like I had learned as a smokejumper. I also found out that several of my old jumper buddies were involved. One in particular was Herm Ball. While I didn't jump with Herm, he was one of the fire staff officers for major fires in my region and as I found out later was my mentor and the person who got me assigned to a fire supervisory job. Herm was also one of the first smokejumpers who worked for the CIA on the Tibetan affair. The CIA recruited smokejumpers to drop cargo to the Tibetans, then later in Laos because of their training and the kind of can-do people they were.

In 1962 and 1963, I continued my design of campgrounds and other recreation sites on the White River National Forest. I also got requests from other forests to do projects for them. I went over to the Arapaho National Forest by Dillon, Colorado, and designed a large complex with over one hundred camping units called Prospector next to Dillon Reservoir, which was under construction. It was the largest site plan I had done but not that complex. My rod man was Pat Lynch, a new employee, who later worked for me on the Dillon District and became a life-long friend. The ranger there didn't have any idea what he wanted so it was up to me. I tried different things, including designing a roundabout. I learned about roundabouts in school and thought it would be fun to try. I left the design with whomever built the site and did not get back to see it until 1965.

The White River National Forest at that time received another large budget for recreation construction, mainly camp and picnic grounds. By this time I had gained the district rangers' confidence and they gave me a free hand, but I always interviewed them to discover what their issues and goals were. In one case I redesigned all the small recreation sites in the Maroon Valley. I then went to the county abstract office and looked up all the mining claim names in the records and picked the ones I thought were catchy. They remain today.

Back in those days there was very little public involvement, so things moved fast. One day Glenwood District Ranger Paul Reedy called and said he had some year-end money he had to spend and wanted to build a parking lot and boat launching site at Sweetwater Lake. We went to the site with a bulldozer following us. We walked the site, I made my recommendation and Paul said, "Let's do it." I started tying ribbons and then got a long stick with a flag and had the bulldozer operator follow me through the oak brush. By the end of the day we had the site roughed out.

Ranger Reedy also asked me to help with his Multiple Use Plan, which the district was required to do based on the Multiple Use Sustained Yield Act of 1961. That was an interesting exercise, but very little planning was necessary. It was mainly drawing lines around existing features, such as streams.

Early in my career I loved to be around horses, riding or packing into the wilderness. I guess this all started on my Uncle Arnold's farm when I was young. He had a Shetland pony that was mean. That pony would go out of his way to bite you, roll over, or buck you off. As time went on I learned how to read his next move. When I got to the White River I was pretty good at handling a horse and the Forest Service gave me a lot of opportunities to do so. During my recreation inventory days of 1959 and 1960 we used horses to visit many of the lakes on the forest to write reports. Many of these trips were overnight so I learned how to pack and manage a string of horses.

When Walt Werner came to work for me, my interest really increased. Walt, being a ranch kid from Colorado, taught me a lot about horses. They are dumb animals and can be spooked for a lot of reasons, so you always needed to be alert. On one trip we took into the Flat Top Primitive Area on an inventory project, we got caught in a late summer snowstorm at around 12,000 feet elevation. The storm was soon a blizzard and we had to drop into the forest for protection. We made it to Marvin Lake, just below timberline. We hobbled our three head of stock and started to unpack our gear. We didn't have a tent, so we decided to use our pack cover, which was lying on the ground covered by snow. Without thinking I shook off the canvas and our horses bolted and even with hobbles on their front legs tore down the valley. The next morning, we followed the horse tracks in the snow on foot and finally found them five miles away up against a Forest Service boundary fence.

It was experiences like these that made me love the Forest Service and its opportunities to enjoy the forests. The White River National Forest was a great training ground and probably my favorite place.

CHAPTER 5

SAVING TRAPPERS LAKE

Trappers Lake, White River National Forest, Colorado
Matthew A. Pearce, in a paper titled "Cradle of the Wilderness," wrote that
Arthur Carhart felt that "there was, in his mind, a higher use for Trappers
Lake, and rightly so." I, too, had the same feeling.

M Y BIGGEST ASSIGNMENT on the White River turned out to be the most historic: Designing recreation developments at Trappers Lake.

Trappers Lake is the second largest natural lake in Colorado, located at the head of the White River on the Meeker District of the White River National Forest. It sits in a large basin surrounded by volcanic cliffs of the White River Plateau. The three-hundred-acre lake has crystal clear water filled with native Colorado Cutthroat Trout. Surrounding the lake are rolling benches covered with Engelmann spruce and open meadows. In the early years of the Forest Service, few people knew of the lake and surrounding wilderness. It is at least as iconic as, say, the Maroon Bells or Mount of the Holy Cross. I can still remember on a crisp, clear and quiet fall morning how the lake reflected the background of the surrounding cliffs. However, for all its beauty and undeveloped wilderness character, Trappers Lake was vulnerable to development from the time the National Forest System was established until the area was finally included in the Flat Top Wilderness Area in 1975.

Arthur Carhart, A Wilderness Advocate

In 1919, a young Forest Service landscape architect by the name of Arthur Carhart, who became a lifelong advocate for wilderness preservation, was sent to Trappers Lake to plan a summer home development and other commercial uses. Summer home developments had been popular during that period. After inventorying the area, he saw how special Trappers Lake was and recommended to his superior, Carl Stahl, who was the regional operations assistant for the U.S. Forest Service in Colorado, that the lake and its surroundings be preserved in its natural state with no man-made developments.

The following quote is from a paper written by Matthew A. Pearce titled "Cradle of the Wilderness, part 1, May 2016," written for the celebration of the passage of the Wilderness Act of 1964. It highlights Arthur Carhart's thoughts on Trappers Lake.

Thus, Arthur Carhart started his survey for the potential construction of cabins and roads around Trappers Lake. As he later commented in his book Timber in Your Life, Carhart grew increasingly troubled as he went to work. "The place was getting a strange hold on me," he wrote, a feeling that he feared would be gone forever if summer homes and automobiles shattered the lake's tranquility. Therefore, he returned to his supervisors in Denver, Colorado, with two suggestions that went on to become important pillars of the modern wilderness movement. First, he proposed that the area immediately surrounding Trappers Lake should remain roadless and free from further development. This reasoning supports the conclusion made by environmental historians that the modern wilderness movement emerged largely in reaction against roads and motorized vehicles. Second, Carhart argued that access to Trappers Lake should remain public. He feared that cars and homes would hinder the enjoyment of the area. Therefore, in addition to recommending against development in the immediate vicinity of Trappers Lake, he proposed certain improvements elsewhere that would facilitate public access to the entire area, including better sanitation, campgrounds, roads, and hiking trails. When examined in this way, Trappers Lake as the "cradle of the wilderness" can be misleading. Carhart did not want to separate the lake from the modern world by preventing the wholesale construction of roads or other developments. Rather, by determining exactly

> where such improvements could be established Carhart tried
> to integrate Trappers Lake with modernity.

His rationale was one of the early concepts of the protection of wild places in the wilderness preservation system that was created by Congress some forty-five years later. The story that has since been told is that this recommendation was accepted.

Trappers Lake Was Not Protected

Mr. Stahl agreed with Arthur that summer home development should not be allowed. However, he took no steps to protect the lake from further development. He had opportunities, in 1929 when the regional forester submitted his recommendation to the chief of the Forest Service, and in 1934 when Mr. Stahl had been promoted to the rank of assistant regional forester for Colorado and the primitive area was designated. Had Trappers Lake been included it would have been protected by regulations that precluded alteration of wilderness areas.

Like Arthur, I was also a boy from Iowa, going to Iowa State University and majoring in landscape architecture. Arthur was the first graduate of that program. From my courses, I knew of Arthur and his recommendations for protection of the Boundary Waters Canoe Area in Minnesota but was not aware of his recommendation to leave Trappers Lake in its natural state.

I first visited the White River National Forest and Trappers Lake in 1959. My crew and I surveyed possible recreation sites around the lake and throughout the entire White River Valley. We hiked and rode horseback around Trappers Lake and into what was then the Flat Top Primitive Area. During this period, there were many millions of acres that were roadless, but only the best of the best were designated as Primitive Areas.

Trappers Lake reminded me of Maroon Lake, which is a portal to the Maroon Bells-Snowmass Wilderness Area outside of Aspen, Colorado. Maroon Lake, like Trappers Lake, was a special place.

What differed is that Maroon Lake already had a road to the end of the lake and development that precluded it for wilderness consideration. My planning recommendation for Maroon Lake removed the road but could not help its wilderness status.

In 1962, I moved on to the planning job at Trappers Lake. My orders from Meeker District Ranger Waldemar Winkler, and my boss Chuck McConnell, the forest recreation forester, were to do a master plan for the lake that would include a resort with a marina, a campground and access roads. The resort owner had been pressing the Forest Service to allow a new resort on the lake, and the small campground across from the resort was in an unattractive setting, inadequate for the use it got, and not suitable for expansion.

There was very little management direction for the area. The White River National Forest 1959 map showed Trappers Lake to be outside of the Flat Top Primitive Area. As far as I knew, a multiple use plan required by the Multiple Use Sustained Yield Act of 1960 had not been done. I had worked on these plans for other districts on the White River National Forest but not for the Meeker District, which included the Trappers Lake area.

Trappers Lake lay in what I assumed would have been the general management zone, a zone that implied that the land management goals were to be established by the Forest Service officer in charge of that piece of land at that time. In other words, Trappers Lake was open for any of the various multiple uses that included man-made developments, such as a resort or a developed campground.

At the time the area got very little public use, mainly fishermen and hunters. It was so isolated that it was difficult to get to; the road below the lake was close to being primitive. A Colorado game and fish hatchery and a small cabin existed along the lake shore. The cove next to the cabin was an excellent place for a resort and marina.

This Place Is Special

By this time, I had a wide variety of experiences with some of the grandest scenic landscapes in the United States. Flying over and jumping into the Bob Marshall and other Primitive Areas in Montana and Idaho exposed me to some of the country's most outstanding wilderness areas . I was now a seasoned backpacker and had spent the last three years on the White River National Forest in outstanding backcountry. While these areas were vast and ecologically diverse, as a landscape architect I was always looking for what I called "special places," such as Maroon Lake nestled between the Pyramid and Maroon Bells peaks. These experiences had broadened my vision of what I could do as a landscape architect in the Forest Service, far beyond what I learned in college. The U.S. Forest Service had been given the task of protecting and enhancing these special places and didn't even recognize them and, at that time, did not know how.

I now had concerns about Trappers Lake, as I had struggled with what to do with the development that had affected Maroon Lake. It's as scenic as Trappers Lake. A resort or any development on Trappers Lake, with its iconic scenic background, would degrade this special place.

I turned my attention to finding a campground location that might be suitable to handle the camping use but not be right next to the lakeshore. In reviewing our surveys of potential recreation sites down the valley from the lake done in 1959 and 1960, I could find none.

During our hiking, we came on a large bench above the lake and to the west. The area looked feasible to put in a sizable recreation site but less desirable for a resort. The development could not be seen from the lake. From the site, you could walk out to a wonderful vista of Trappers Lake and the Flat Top's cliffs. It would provide access via a short trail to the lake, which would preclude motorized boat access and be an excellent portal to the primitive area trail system.

Standing on the Trappers Lake overlook in 1962
This overlook, is where I recommended to my boss, Chuck McConnell, that we not build a road, resort, or marina on the shoreline of Trappers Lake. That recommendation was approved.

I took my boss Chuck McConnel to the area and we walked the resort and campground locations I had surveyed. I told him I recommended for the campground but against the resort. The last thing I wanted to do was to downgrade the scenic quality that Trappers Lake offered. As I found out only recently, after reading Thomas Wolf's book, *Arthur Carhart: Wilderness Prophet*, Arthur made a similar argument. At the time Arthur was not thinking of wilderness or of precluding inappropriate development. He was trying to protect a scenic wonder for the public to enjoy without unnecessary distractions.

The last thing I did was walk McConnell out to the overlook we had discovered, and he was sold. He indicated he would also recommend against the resort on the lake but to go with the campground as our preferred option.

Back in the Glenwood Springs, Colorado, forest supervisor's office, I took pains to draw a colorful master plan, with photos of the lake. After my confrontation with staff over my recommendation to eliminate the road along Maroon Lake, I spent time crafting my arguments. The campground was approved but not the resort. I immediately started doing the design and field layout. The campground construction started soon afterward, about 1964.

In 1965, I got a call from the office of Regional Forester Dave Nordwall saying he wanted to see me. I was now the landscape architect on the Arapaho National Forest in Golden, Colorado, just down the street from the regional office in Lakewood. I went to Nordwall's office. He said Arthur Carhart had been there and became upset when he saw the plan for a resort and campground on Trappers Lake. In fact, he wrote a letter to Nordwall expressing his displeasure with the Forest Service over their management of the lake.

That plan was my colored presentation, on an easel, to show the public what kind of recreation planning the Forest Service was doing. I told him the resort portion of the plan was never approved, and a decision by the forest supervisor had precluded any development around the shore. He asked me to contact

Arthur and tell him my story. I was unsuccessful in reaching him.

I did talk to my boss Mike Penfold, the forest recreation and lands staff officer, about the situation. Mike and his father Joe Penfold, who had been the conservation director for the Isaak Walton League, were close friends of Arthur's. In fact, Mike used to stay with him when he came down to Denver from Colorado State College. I thought after that conversation Mike might have called him, but I contacted Mike while writing this memoir and he said he never did.

After the meeting with the regional forester, the incident perked my interest in Arthur's writings. I combed the Forest Service files and came on his report on Trappers Lake, then another report on Mount Evans located outside of Denver. I also read some of his books and other articles I got from a friend, Kay Collins, from the Denver Public Library, about national forest issues. Arthur is billed as a preservationist but the report on Mount Evans and his writings lead me to believe, as a landscape architect, he was true to his profession. In the Mount Evans report he talked about the emergence of the automobile and the need to provide the public opportunities to be able to drive to and enjoy the great outdoors. He even advocated for a tramway to the top of the mountain, so the people of Denver could enjoy it. His philosophy was not to discourage development but to provide a balance of different uses, including wilderness, in such a way that the inherent values of the forest were not destroyed. Years later I found that he was also an advocate of public and private partnerships for recreation development on public lands, such as ski areas. He could have advocated for the cabins but there was, in his mind, a higher use for Trappers Lake. Rightly so.

Why Was Trappers Lake Not Protected?

When I think back on Trappers Lake, it is a small wonder it remained primitive. There were, over the decades, demands that could have changed the lake's character. In his writings, Arthur understood the fact that at any time a decision could be rendered that would allow degrading development. As he said in his book, *The National Forests*, "Most of the wilderness within the national forests, unfortunately, are [*sic*] in constant jeopardy."

In researching this subject, I came on two different maps of the Flat Top Primitive Area. The first map, along with the proposed management direction, was signed by the regional forester in 1929 and submitted to the chief of the Forest Service. The area was then listed at 117,000 acres and the boundary excluded the lake but was along a portion of the east shoreline of the lake ending at the cove where the Colorado game & fish department fish hatchery was located. The Flat Top Primitive Area, when created by the chief in 1934, was 118,230 acres in size and Trappers Lake was left outside of the area. The boundary was moved to above the lake on the cliffs. The reasons for the different boundary locations are not documented. There may be several reasons.

The report sent to Washington with the regional forester's recommendation mentioned that there was timber available in the area. When I designed the campground west of the lake, the area was covered with a large stand of mature old growth Engelmann spruce. It was dead in 1961 from a spruce bud worm epidemic but was green timber in 1929 and valuable for lumber.

The area boundary on the east side of the lake ran right along the shoreline and then turned away to the east when it reached the game and fish hatchery. It suggests that the state of Colorado may not have wanted the lake included because of their fish management objectives. Fish culture activities, at that

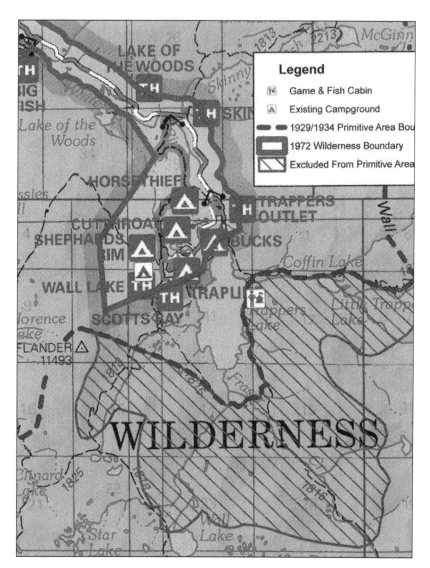

Changes in Trappers Lake area, 1929–1972

time, were forbidden in the primitive area's proposed management plan.

The further mystery is why was the boundary moved away from Trappers Lake to the top of the cliffs in the final Flat Top Primitive Area decision in 1934?

As it turned out, the Bureau of Reclamation showed interest in Trappers Lake as a possible reservoir site and the boundary along the lakeshore would interfere. Sometime around 1929 they withdrew Trappers Lake from consideration for primitive area designation when they determined it was a possible reservoir site. There were later reports that it would not be a good site for a dam. The bureau officially dropped their interest in 1964 when the Wilderness Act was passed by Congress.

No doubt Arthur's recommendations were very important, especially planting the seed for future wilderness protection. When I first visited the area in 1959 the Flat Top Primitive Area boundary was located at the top of the cliffs, excluding Trappers Lake. I was on a path that would have precluded it from Wilderness designation. In looking at the final Wilderness boundary it went around the campground I designed. When I did my design that area could also have qualified for Wilderness.

The Forest Service recommended 142,230 acres for wilderness designation for the Flat Top in 1967. It excluded qualified acreage adjacent to the Primitive Area based on objections from water users, mineral and the timber industry, but now included Trappers Lake. Other public input wanted more acres included and the final recommendation and designation was 235,214 acres, which was approved by Congress.

Saving Trappers Lake from being eliminated for Wilderness designation seems to have been a team effort: Arthur Carhart's vision and recommendation in 1919 to leave the lake in its natural condition; the decision by the White River National Forest in 1962 to not authorize a resort or a campground on the lakeshore; and the Bureau of Reclamation dropping their interest in a reservoir site in 1964. The Flat Top Primitive Area, including the addition of Trappers Lake, was added to the Wilderness system in 1975.

The appropriate and lasting decision was finally made.

CHAPTER 6

THE FRYINGPAN DISTRICT

Photo courtesy of the U.S. Forest Service

Ruedi Reservoir on the Fryingpan River, near Basalt, Colorado

M Y LAST ASSIGNMENT on the White River was on the Fryingpan District. The Bureau of Reclamation was building Ruedi Reservoir up the Frying Pan River out of Basalt, Colorado. Ruedi Reservoir was part of the Fryingpan-Arkansas Project, which was designed to divert water from the west slope of Colorado to the east slope. The reservoir was built on public lands, with the lands above the highwater line to be managed by the Forest Service.

The forest supervisor on the forest at that time was Ken Schulz, and he decided I should transfer to the district office and coordinate the master planning and design of the recreation facilities that were to be built. This was in 1963. I was, as far as I know, the first landscape architect to be assigned to a district position full time. I was also promoted to a GS-9.

This did provide a hardship for me because I had a nice rental home at the base of Storm King Mountain outside of Glenwood Springs and there was nothing available in Basalt because of the construction workers. The Fryingpan District Ranger, Dick Serino, insisted I move to be able to respond to forest fires on short notice. I finally found one room in a basement.

Most of my involvement was with the Bureau of Reclamation staff out of Pueblo, Colorado. It was there I met and worked with Harold Sersland. We became good friends. Harold was a forestry graduate from the University of Minnesota, had played hockey for the university and was an excellent skier. He was an immense help to me, as I knew very little about large reservoir recreation development.

The first thing Harold did was organize trips to all the big reservoirs that had facilities already built or under construction. I lined up the Forest Service plane out of Denver and several of us, flew to Flaming Gorge in Utah and Glen Canyon in Arizona and Utah. We got tours from the Bureau and the National Park Service and were able to talk to their design engineers. Harold and I also visited several reservoirs on the Great Plains.

I later moved from my basement apartment to a trailer close to the Ranger Station. One night we had a tremendous snow storm. While I was walking to work, I looked up at Serino's window and there sat a pair of ski boots. Back home I went to get my gear, and off we went to Aspen. We arrived at Aspen Highlands Ski Area before the lifts opened. The operator let us on the lift and said, "The crew is up on the mountain shooting avalanches and you can join them." It had snowed fifty inches the night before. As we approached the steep slope, we heard an explosion above us high on the mountain. The next thing we knew, we heard a roar heading our way. Even though the area was heavily forested we could see a cloud of snow coming down on us. "Hold on," Dick yelled. The blast hit us with such a force that we were horizontal to the ground. The snow was below us but there were trees and brush flying through the air. We swung back and forth but the cable didn't come off its support and we were OK. We continued to the top and found that the snow was so deep we had to walk our way down no matter how steep the slope was. That was my first encounter with an avalanche.

As I gained more experience as a landscape architect I was called on various times for my input on ski area feasibility studies. On the Fryingpan District, we had a potential ski area above Ruedi Reservoir. Fritz Benedict, an architect out of Aspen, wanted to go up the mountain with a couple developers to show them the ski terrain. The ranger and I were included. We were towed behind a snowmobile going up the mountain. When we got to the top, the snowmobile broke down. It was getting late in the day and our snowmobile operator didn't have skis or snowshoes to get off the mountain. We were not prepared to stay overnight. I volunteered to ski down and call for help. It was an eerie experience. I was skiing though the trees with very little moonlight. I narrowly missed a fence and almost went over a cliff. I finally made the road and still had a couple of miles to go to the nearest ranch. I made it by midnight. I called the forest staff officer, Paul Hauck, and he started the rescue.

Later that night the rest of the group came off the mountain just as the rescue team arrived. "How did you get off?" I asked. It turns out Mr. Benedict had been a 10th Mountain trouper with the army. They taught the soldiers how to make a ski rescue with two people on one set of skis. He had skied the snowmobile operator off the mountain on the back of his skis.

Back on the district, I hired several landscape architecture students and we proceeded with the master plan and started on the detail design for the reservoir. One day we got a call saying that Chief of the Forest Service, Ed Cliff, the regional forester, and the forest supervisor were coming to the district office to review our work. They were to arrive on a Saturday morning for a presentation, which I would be giving at 9:00. This presented a major problem for me.

Saturday was the opening of turkey season, and my friend Bob Veltus had arranged for us to hunt on a private ranch. I told him I would have to rush. Well, I shot the biggest gobbler I have ever gotten but I was pressed for time. Still in hunting clothes, with blood on my pants, I raced to the office to find the folks all waiting for me in the conference room. I arrived just in time. I gave my presentation, and all went well. Ed Cliff was most interested in my turkey hunt and wanted to see the bird.

My last year on the White River, I got another fire call for a fire in the Glenwood District along the edge of the Flat Top Primitive Area. When I arrived, my job was to take a crew of Hopis to the fire for night duty. We were to be transported by helicopter with the pilot taking two firefighters at a time. I was standing on the porch of a Forest Service guard station eating a sandwich while watching the crew get on the copter. For some reason the pilot changed his approach from south to north. Before my eyes, a young Hopi tucked his head down and ran into the tail rotor head first. I immediately grabbed a tarp and threw it over him. It was a brutal injury and he died instantly.

Given this loss, the fire boss wanted to have the Hopi crew leader taken back to the fire and then bring all the fire crew back to fire camp. I was assigned the task of taking the crew leader in a jeep to the fire. I had been to the area when I was doing recreation survey work back in 1959. I remembered it as the roughest four-wheel drive road I had ever been on, five miles of boulders. The crew leader and I started out at sunset. He didn't speak English but was having a great time on the road, constantly laughing with a toothless grin. When we arrived in the dark he gathered the crew together and told them the sad news of their crew member's death. I said we need to start walking out. They all said no, they wanted to work.

Later in the evening I asked one of the crew who could speak English why they seemed unconcerned. He said they all needed the money and didn't know the person that well. It seems they came from all parts of their reservation in Arizona and never saw each other except for fire duty.

To this day, I blame myself for the Hopi boy's death. I had been an air officer on fires and knew that there should have been someone posted by those young men as they approached the helicopter to ensure they made the right approach. While that was the fire boss's decision, I should have done something.

When I hear people complaining about Forest Service fire-fighting efforts on major fires I wish they could live through what I did. On wildfires, everyone on the line is in jeopardy.

My last design job on the White River was a detail to the Pike National Forest located in Colorado Springs, Colorado. I worked with their landscape architect on a design for the old Monument nursery site. It was no longer needed. While a nice location, the site was already being encroached upon by development. It was close to the Air Force Academy and prime property for development. We designed a high-end destination campground for trailer parking. The site never did get built, and I'm not sure how it ended up.

The most interesting thing about this detail is that while I was there, in the spring of 1964, Colorado Springs had a huge flood that isolated the town and blocked all the roads. I sat there for almost a week before I could get out of town. Many years later one of my future bosses, Steve Yurich, told me he lost all his household goods in that flood. He was in the process of moving from Wyoming to Denver and had his belongings stored in a warehouse along the South Platte River in Denver.

Towards the end of the summer, we were fine-tuning our recreation designs for the reservoir development when I was offered the job as the landscape architect for the Arapaho National Forest located in Golden, Colorado. It was a promotion to a GS-11.

CHAPTER 7

ARAPAHO NATIONAL FOREST AND RECREATION DESIGN

Dillon Reservoir

Dillon Reservoir is an outstanding recreation area west of Denver, Colorado. I had the opportunity to plan, design, and supervise construction of all the National Forest recreation sites around the reservoir including the marina shown in the foreground.

IT WAS NOW SEPTEMBER of 1964, and I moved to Golden, Colorado, and my new job. This was a great challenge as I would have the opportunity to design all the facilities at Dillon Reservoir, get involved in ski area development and feasibility studies, and be the staff assistant in charge of the recreation management program for the forest. Again, I would be the first landscape architect they had ever hired.

The person I replaced had not been well liked by the district's rangers. In fact, one ranger threw this individual out of his office into a snowbank and told him never to come back. When the rangers got together they said they were not going to listen to a landscape architect. I was told this by Neil Edstrom, who had moved from the Aspen District on the White River to the district ranger job on the Clear Creek District. Neil and I had become close friends, and he defended me. He said, "Jim's OK and he can out-ski all of you." They gave me a chance and it worked out fine.

The timber staff officer on the forest was Gordon Brown, the district ranger I worked for on my first summer job with the Forest Service in Saratoga, Wyoming. It was because of Gordon that I was accepted into the smokejumping program. When I thanked him again, his response was cool. Behind his desk, he had an enlarged photo of the timber clear-cuts on his old district, which he was very proud of. The cuts ran in straight blocks up the mountain side. He must have thought because I was a landscape architect I would look negatively on his work. If I had learned anything working with the Forest Service, it was that as an outsider the way to make change was not by being negative.

My boss at that time was Bob Scholz. Bob was the lands and recreation staff officer for the Arapaho National Forest. He was also the brother of Ken Scholz, who was the forest supervisor on the White River National Forest and the person who transferred and promoted me to the Fryingpan District. Ken must have spoken well of me.

Bob was known as being a tough boss. The other staff members working for him told me he never accepted a letter written by them without major corrections. Having been a company clerk for a while in the army, I knew how small errors could cause a letter to be redone several times. I worked extra hard on my first correspondence and handed it in to Bob. Later he came to my desk threw the letter down, said, "Good job," and left.

Bob left me alone. I had my hands full lining out my work on Dillon Reservoir. Except for the campground I had designed several years earlier, Prospector, the rest of the recreation sites and the lake's marinas had yet to be designed let alone built. Bob took me out to get an overview of the area but first drove me over to Prospector. As I mentioned earlier, I had designed a roundabout at that campground. Bob had a tough time with this feature and kept going around it in circles. He said, "Whoever designed this thing is an idiot." He asked me if I could correct this mess. I said, "Sure, no problem." I never told him I was the idiot.

I got along well with the district rangers but did have an issue with Howard Kelso, the forest engineer. Howard had moved from the White River to the Arapaho National Forest a couple of years before I did. Neil Edstrom, the Clear Creek District ranger, called me and wanted me to look at a campground road design Howard's staff had done. Neil felt the road was overdesigned for the area and would cause him problems. I agreed and proceeded to pull all the survey stakes up. The road foreman told Kelso and my boss Bob Scholz. They were upset with me. I suggested to

Howard that he assign Tom Edwards, a civil engineer, to work with me. We got along and worked as a team. Heaton Bay Campground on the Dillon District was probably the best design we did. I wanted the roads to sit lightly on the land and use cuts and fills to control traffic rather than concrete or log barriers.

By this time I had designed so many campgrounds with several hundred campsites that I had lost count. Thrown into these designs were marinas, overlooks, picnic grounds, and other small sites. One of the fun and different sites was a camp and picnic ground on an island in Dillon Reservoir near Heaton Bay Campground. It provided a unique challenge in managing the site, particularly how the toilets would be pumped out and the sewage taken ashore. The Denver Water Board staff was very concerned with this development, because the reservoir helped supply drinking water to Denver. After many meetings and proposals everyone agreed on a barge with a sealed tank to haul the sewage to shore. The Dillon District now had a navy.

During this time, I hired landscape architecture students during the summer to help do small design jobs and details. Several of these people, such as Doug Pederson and Jurgen Hess, were excellent help and went on to pursue a career in the Forest Service..

The biggest design challenge was the marinas on the reservoir. Both communities next to the reservoir wanted marinas. The town of Dillon, Colorado, was at the lower end of the reservoir and close to the dam. It had the deepest water and could support a marina with the high water-level fluctuation anticipated. The town of Frisco, Colorado was at the upper end of the reservoir with shallow water levels. In its case, a water fluctuation would create a mud flat. From my experience at Ruedi Reservoir and what I learned working with the Bureau of Reclamation engineers, the Frisco location would cause significant problems for anyone investing in a marina operation. The issue was political, especially in Frisco and with some of the Forest Service personnel. I called my friend Harold Sersland in the Bureau of Reclamation and arranged for a trip back out to Flaming Gore Reservoir in Utah and Glen Canyon in Arizona. The Forest Service and Park Service staff we visited convinced our staff to avoid the Frisco location.

I was still in the process of designing the recreation complex at Peak One, which was across the bay from Frisco. The design included a boat launching site that would be close to the town. It would not support a full marina operation but could be used during high water in the reservoir. It turned out this site became very popular with trailer users and the parking lot would fill up every weekend. Dillon Reservoir is normally left full, causing the reservoir to appear to be a natural lake. Eventually, the town of Frisco got its marina, but in 2018 the Denver Water Board needed the water. The boats were then left high and dry.

During the time I was working on recreation areas, I was also getting involved in ski area feasibility studies and management. The Arapaho National Forest at that time had several ski areas on national forest lands and more being considered. The older areas like Winter Park near Granby, Colorado; Berthoud Pass, a weekend area at the top of the pass; Loveland Ski Area at the east base of Loveland Pass; and Arapaho Basin on the west side of the pass were going strong. The Breckenridge Ski Area (outside of Breckenridge, Colorado) was under new ownership and was planning expansion. With my background in landscape architecture, the Forest Service called on my expertise to work with the permittees on everything from site design to base area development. One of these potential permittees was a resort owner by the name of Max Durham. He had been promoting an area called Keystone. Working with Max afforded me the opportunity to expand my skills and do what I loved most at that time: ski.

I averaged at least sixty days a year on skis. Some for work and a lot for play. I would take all my vacation time visiting ski areas throughout the West. Colorado skiing is some of the best in the world, but my favorite area was Alta in Utah. I went to all the Forest Service schools on avalanche control to improve my skiing. Some weekends I would volunteer to do avalanche control at Berthoud Pass. The Forest Service did the control work for that area.

All this effort paid off, as I now got the opportunity to do ski area feasibility studies for the Forest Service. With the advent of skiing and the building of mega-areas such as Vail and Snowmass, every mountain that had private land at its base was being proposed as a ski area. Developers saw riches in ski area development and related land sales. The forest supervisor commissioned me to do a study of potential ski areas in northern Colorado. That resulted in a report on each area and a written description of its potential. Most were not feasible for a variety of reasons. There were a couple of exceptions: Keystone and Copper Mountain, both in Summit County, Colorado.

I spent many days on a snowmobile or in a snowcat going up Keystone with Max Durham. He was a wonderful man to get acquainted with and was dedicated to Keystone becoming a great area. What he lacked was financial backing. There was a group of men who would come to Colorado from Cedar Rapids, Iowa, to ski. They stayed at Max's lodge and Max convinced them Keystone would be a great ski area. They eventually convinced Ralston Purina to invest in the area, and it opened in the late 1960s.

The other area I supported in my studies was Copper Mountain. In my report on potential ski areas in Colorado, I wrote a glowing report about the area's potential as a ski area. The area quoted my writeup in its first brochure.

"If there was a mountain that had terrain for skiing it would be Copper Mountain. It is probably the most outstanding potential ski area in the Arapaho National Forest, and possibly in Colorado. The north-facing peaks of Copper Mountain offer an excellent variety of development for expert, intermediate, and beginner skiers. The mountain has good snow and the sparse tree cover, created by old burns, which offers a tremendous opportunity to create natural-type runs that blend in with the surrounding countryside."

The area opened in 1972, the year I moved to Denver from Summit County. Chuck Lewis was the person behind Copper Mountain's development. Chuck was an excellent businessman, a visionary, and a real gentleman.

One area I did a feasibility study on was down the Blue River in Summit County. It was located next to a ranch owned by David and Susan Ray. I spent time climbing the mountain in both the summer and winter. It had some potential but had many issues. I believe David knew the outcome of my report, but he didn't take it personally. In fact, we became friends, which benefited me in later years.

CHAPTER 8

SNEAK POINT: A FOREST FIRE

Photo courtesy of Mike McMillan

A typical forest fire racing up a ridge line

D URING THE YEARS I fought forest fires, there were two exceptional years when the forests of Montana and Idaho had several large fires: 1961 and 1967. In both cases I was detailed from Region 2 in Colorado to be on overhead teams to manage fires. Both fires I was on were in Idaho on the Clearwater National Forest. The 1967 fire, Sneak Point, was the largest and most difficult fire I was ever on. This is its story, adapted from the report I recorded in 1968.

Our sixteen-man overhead team, a team of firefighting specialists trained to take a command role in managing large forest fires, had spent a weary twenty-four hours traveling from Denver, Colorado, to Orofino, Idaho. Ralph Johnson and I received our fire call at three o'clock Friday afternoon, packed our gear, and headed for the airport. Other team members had arrived, some old friends, some new. Wayne Cook was our fire

All but two of Region 2's overhead team; the arrow points to me

boss and Herm Ball, another former Missoula smokejumper, was one of his assistants. Our flight turned out to be a battled-tested DC-3 that, after takeoff, developed engine trouble over Wyoming and we all returned to Denver. The region's chief pilot then started to shuttle our team, five at a time, to Missoula, Montana in a Forest Service Beechcraft Bonanza.

Missoula looked as if it was ready for war. The airport was lined with aircraft; not the slick modern aircraft of the military but old tri-motors, twin airs, and twin Beechcrafts for the smokejumpers; World War II bombers and fighters used to drop chemical retardant on fires; and a variety of small aircraft for spotting and observation. On the horizon, sleek airline passenger flights landed one after another filled with firefighters from around the country.

The atmosphere and talk were gay, but we were tense with the anticipation of the unknown. Before we had much time to think about it someone yelled for our team, "Grab your things and board that bus, you're going to Idaho, somewhere outside of Orofino, Sneak Point." The fire was on the North Fork of the Clearwater River and in some of the roughest country around.

Hours later we arrived at our fire camp, very tired and disorganized. We were a team in name only with no job assignment and no idea where we were. I don't believe District Ranger Jim Jordan knew we were coming or what to do with us. He had several fires burning on his district and this one was a monster.

Sneak Point is a prominent point in otherwise uninteresting country. The fire camp was below the point and above the fire raging below. What we didn't realize is that a short way out on the ridge the canyon of the Clearwater River plunged two thousand feet covered with flammable brush, big timber and goat rocks—called that because goats are the only animals crazy enough to live in them. The fire was already in the rocks, and looking at the flames, the steepness of the terrain, and all-around potential for tragedy, it made us feel like we had already lost.

The fire had started as loggers hauled logs away from one of their cuts. The weather was so hot and dry that friction from a cable being dragged across a dead stump caused the wood to burst into flames. Within minutes the small flame spurted to life and roared through the newly cut timber, quickly destroying three hundred acres. From there the fire ran wild.

We bedded down for the night in anticipation of the next day. That morning, dawn broke with an inversion of layers of smoke like fog obscuring our vision. Everything was still, and our eyes burned. Even though we couldn't see a thing the weather was a blessing, as the conditions kept the fire quiet for a day while we came to our senses.

We trudged through an almost mystical world of gray. Smokejumpers and district crews had already started a fire line down one side of the fire. A fire line is a line of bare ground that a fire can't burn though. The unburned forest sat shrouded in a smoky mist while next to our line the fire had blackened every living thing. The tall ghosts of burned trees still smoked and belched fire.

Occasionally one of these trees would burn through and come crashing down. A cry would go out "Snag!" and all eyes would search the mist for movement. The fear of instant death hung over us and made everyone tense. The slope was so steep that as the snag would fall it turned into a missile shooting down the mountain, swift, silent like a bowling ball heading for a strike. First a moment of rushing noise, then a crash and silence.

Deadly burned trees silently fly down the mountain like bowling balls

How do we fight this monster? It was decided the first day we would get acquainted with the firefighters already on the fire line and become familiar with the terrain and movement of the flames. The fire was divided into two divisions, one side where the timber was big, and a small creek offered a starting point for controlling the blaze, and the other side above the river and in the goat rocks. Within each division would be sectors of approximately one-quarter to one-half mile each. Each sector had several crews of firefighters. My assignment was as the division boss in charge of the section with the big timber, which became known as "the hole." I hiked down to meet the men already on the line and ran into Dave, the present division boss I was to replace. It turned out Dave had been a smokejumper out of McCall, Idaho and knew his business. The rest of the first day I spent with Dave checking the crew's progress and assessing our situation. It was depressing.

The upper half of the division was safe, but as we dropped down into the canyon towards a small creek, snags were falling constantly. Higher up on the mountain we could hear the fire roaring as the afternoon heated up. Below us were huge white pines and thick brush, a potential trap that the fire could use to cook us alive in one rush. Fortunately, the inversion held in the valley bottom and our crew reached the river without too many problems.

I say, not too many problems. The creek bottom was steep, and a few men took bad spills. The dry weather had also caused the insect population to explode, and we were constantly harassed. Ralph Johnson, now one of my sector bosses, took a fall and landed in a yellowjacket nest. He hurt on both ends and suffered for the rest of the fire. As if this was not enough, one of the Spanish-American crews had never been on a big fire like this and they were scared to death. They didn't like snags sneaking up on them—who did?

We changed our fire bosses' plan and moved our line-building to the upper side of the creek away from the fire above us. This would end up burning some prized white pine stands but would let us use the creek as a barrier from the snags screaming down the mountain on top of us. The only issue was we had to back burn from our new line position to the creek, not an easy task. Back burns are when you burn existing vegetation to create a buffer between your position and the wild fire. There was enough water in the creek that we could set up pumps and were able to control our back burns as we inched toward the river. The decision had been made, but our daylight was running out and I needed to get over one hundred men out of there for the night. We didn't have any relief help, extra food, or drinking water.

We trudged down to the river and for the first time we got a look at the Clearwater, a stone's throw wide with deep holes and rapids.

The road to safety lay on the other side of the river, where the buses would meet us to take us back to fire camp. I had been around water all my life and just assumed we would swim across. Then I saw the shocked faces of the Native American crews. They were Navajos and Zuni from the desert in Arizona. They sat down and said, "No wade." The young men were eager for the experience but not their elders. I yelled on the radio for fire camp, "Tell them we need a boat." Fire camp answered, "You got to be kidding, a boat? Your buses will be there in half an hour. Wade the river."

It was only when the younger men took the arms of the elders that we coaxed them across the river. We begged, pleaded and finally—after dragging three quarters of the men—got

Crossing the North Fork of the Clearwater—slippery rocks and deep holes

everyone across. Another two hours on a school bus and we were back at fire camp. At 10:00 P.M. we ate dinner, almost falling asleep doing it. Our first day had ended.

At three o'clock in the morning I thought I was dreaming that I was being kicked off the mountain. It wasn't a dream. They were kicking my sleeping bag and yelling "Rise and shine!" Someone had decided we should get an early start. It was early all right, and I could still remember in 1961 when the men on the Horseshoe Lake Fire had walked off the job because of ill treatment. Working for the Forest Service I had no choice, but if we lost our locals and the Native American crews we had problems. A quick complaint to the fire boss, Wayne, put a stop to this nonsense. Fighting fires is a lot like the army. The men take a tremendous physical and mental beating on the fire line that many of the backup people and public cannot understand. We were thankful our support team was giving us everything we needed, except boats. The supply section was up all night sharpening implements, arranging transportation when we needed it and cooking meals. Our cooks were ladies from the local communities who provided us with tremendous meals under adverse conditions. The local logging industry gave us all the help it could, as we found out later that morning.

At 5:00 A.M. the crews assembled to head for our assignments. A call had gone out to the community that we needed sawyers and over forty showed up to help. The men were a tough lot. They didn't exactly love the Forest Service, but they respected our firefighting knowledge—at least if you could prove to them you knew what you were talking about. We divided them into teams with the sawyers for felling the trees and each with a helper. We then headed into "the hole."

I had picked up a helper, Al. He was an assistant ranger on an adjacent Forest Service district. He was a big, raw-boned guy with lots of fire experience. I put him in charge of managing our back fires when we used that strategy. Together we started another suspense-filled day of falling snags, flames, heat, wasps, and that blasted river crossing.

Grif and Ralph were my two sector bosses. Grif's crews built a line down the creek, and Ralph's crews controlled the backfires Al had set. Our little endeavor could easily backfire on us if we didn't burn out small areas at a time. The foliage was so dry, even the heat of the fire could start another fire across our line. Ralph kept the men busy soaking down the unburned side of our fire line, even using their hard hats to carry water. The loggers were busy felling dead standing trees next to our line for fear they would ignite and send sparks to the unburned side. As much good as this did, it provided enough fuel to keep the fire raging, but at least it was controlled.

Our once clear and beautiful bubbling stream had now turned black with soot. We were amazed to find a few fish, but they would soon be dead. The devastation to wildlife was becoming apparent to all of us. One logger, a big tough-looking guy, was trying to hide the tears coming down his face. He had just seen two squirrels burn to death in their treetop home.

Suddenly the radio barked, "We're trapped and there is no way out but over the cliffs." It was John, one of the sector bosses on the other division. His assignment had been to go over the goat rocks and tie his line into my division coming up from the river. As he worked down through the rocks he ran into the cliffs. In the meantime, the inversion had lifted, and the fire came alive in a big way. Where only occasional trees had torched out now groups of trees started blowing up in flames and the fire ran from tree to tree with explosive fury. John was safe in the rocks, but the fire had cut off his retreat. His only escape was to work his way down the cliffs. He had already had one man hurt from a falling rock and was scared to risk more injuries. As they made their descent we kept giving them encouragement, but it was going to take a while to make that climb.

I had almost forgotten about Ralph and his crews. He came trudging down to say he almost lost the line. When the inversion lifted, the fire, including our backfires, started burning like the very devil was fanning them. He had spent the day just trying to hold on.

Evening was upon us and the wind and fire became quiet. John had finally made it off the side of the mountain without anyone else getting hurt in the cliffs. The air along the river was rapidly cooling and the crews were wading the river this time without trouble. That is all except the loggers. They had a special problem. They were carrying heavy power saws and other equipment and were trying to keep it dry. Most of them had made it when suddenly one older man lost his footing and tumbled into the rapids, which swept him into deep water. He couldn't swim but the quick thinking of two other young loggers came to his rescue. One jumped in and grabbed the old logger by one hand while the other extended an axe handle for the other young logger to grab. With a lurch both men pulled the man from the deep water until he could regain his feet. Another close call. We again requested boats but to no avail.

During the night, a Forest Service plane flew over the fire, taking infra-red pictures. At the time this was a new technique to plot the fire activity and location. From the information, our fire behavior expert and fire boss decided on what they thought was a coup de grace.

In the gray light of dawn, sleepy eyes and all, I found out I had been appointed the executioner. They had changed divisions on me and I now had the goat rocks and cliffs. We were to send one crew of fifty men up a ravine from the river building a line. Two crews of Native Americans would come off the top, one building a line down a ridge to the ravine and the other burning out the brush from our line to the fire. The other division would go into "the hole" to continue burning out from the creek where I had been the day before. It seemed like a trap, but I was too speechless to object. But not John, one of our sector bosses. After being trapped in the rocks and cliffs the day before he wanted no part of this plan. Wayne, our fire boss, would not give in. It was this or burn off three hundred acres of prized white pine timber that the forest supervisor wanted to save.

The top of the fire was in less steep terrain, and caterpillar tractors were being used to build the fire lines. From the end of the cat line we walked out on the rocks. For the first time, I looked over into the canyon, fifteen hundred feet below I could see the North Fork of the Clearwater River winding its way through the canyon. We all started down, carefully picking our way through the rocks. One group would work its way over the cliffs keeping close together. When they reached a safe spot, another group would start. Occasionally rocks would jar loose and go rumbling down the mountainside. During one of these rock storms I got a call from Al. He said a missile had just missed his head and an Native American had been hit. It was very dangerous, and I was afraid someone would be seriously hurt. Everyone was tense, and our day wore on slowly. I remembered my experience during my first fire jump when our crew got caught in a rock slide on the Pine Creek Fire. We were saved because we had a lookout to give us warning. I ordered lookouts for our descent.

We made some mistakes that day that slowed our progress. We had underestimated the difficulty of the task. The line was not complete. The men had run out of drinking water. It was three o'clock in the afternoon, and I still had to create a clearing so the night crew could monitor the fire's progress. After a long trip to the river for water we started the clearing.

Suddenly came the cry, "Rock!" Our lookouts were screaming at the top of their lungs. For years, the vegetation had held back the loose rocks and now that the vegetation was burned it freed them to bombard us. "Rock, Rock" pierced the silence again striking terror into our hearts. We were trapped in this narrow gulley with no escape. We had a spilt second to dive for cover. I glanced up to see boulders the size of barrels flying parallel to the ground. They flew over our heads and smashed into other rocks. Fortunately, everyone was all right and we worked our way down to the river to end another long day.

That night the infrared flight had shown our line held. We hoped the next day we would gain control. The fire had other ideas.

The next morning at briefing the weather man gave us a warning. Winds up to thirty-five miles per hour were expected with gusts up to fifty by noon. We had until noon to finish burning out our line. The fire spent the night "cooling it" but as morning heated up it started to rage. We could hear the roar above us. Smoke was blackening the sky. We were having trouble with our back burns down next to the gully. I figured our only chance of burning out the line was to go above the gully where the vegetation was dryer to start the back burn. Hopefully this would cause the upper fire to draw the fires along the gully together. It was nerve-racking as now we were in an unburned area with fires above and below us.

Disaster! We were so effective that the whole mountain exploded in flames. At the same time the weather front hit us with terrific up-canyon winds. Within seconds we were surrounded by fire. "To the river!" we yelled. "Back down to the river!" Everyone ran heads down and hands over faces though the flames to safety. The fire had gone wild, suddenly jumping our line and throwing flames hundreds of feet high. We started backing toward the river. We kept hoses trained behind us and on our flanks to give us some protection. It was a mob scene with over a hundred men starting to crowd up as we approached the river.

The fire was now turning into a devastating holocaust. Flames were shooting skyward and a column of smoke rose thousands of feet above the mountains into the atmosphere and darkened the sun. This was no ordinary blowup; everything had a swirling motion. We realized we were witnessing a firestorm. Fingers of fire were racing in different directions with unbelievable velocity. This all happened in the space of a few minutes. Now the entire forest was engulfed in flames and there was a hideous roar like a freight train. Most of my division's crews were bunched up moving toward the river, but one Native American crew was trapped somewhere above us in the smoke. We feared the worst. We were yelling over the radio trying to contact the trapped men, to no avail.

My sector boss Ralph Johnson was managing the easier top section of the line, far up on the canyon top. He was now greeting the fire racing uphill. Later he told me he had been relaxing one moment and the next was facing a wall of fire. He and his crew made a heroic stand and held their line. As they were struggling with the flames a huge black bear came bursting out of the trees and ran right by the men as if they weren't there. The fire then changed directions and raced up the canyon turning several hundred acres into black ash.

Just then we heard from the trapped crew. They had seen the blowup coming and ran back into the area that had already burned off and was cold. The smoke almost choked them, but they could work away from the fire and climb to safety in the cliffs. They were physically exhausted and had almost lost their lives to the fire, but they made it to the top.

We somehow got everyone across the river. I held back the Forest Service management personnel until last. We pitched our tools into the river and dove in to swim across. We laid on the opposite beach watching the fire burn until the buses arrived to take us back to fire camp.

We had lost the day and returned to camp disheartened and weary. It looked as if this fire was on its way to making national headlines, for it had thousands of acres in which to run wild.

The next morning, we had given up. That is, all except the fire boss, Wayne. He had another fantastic plan. The last one had almost lost us several men, so we wanted no part of this one. He kept patting us on the back and telling us we could do it. He admitted the last plan was a wild stab, but we had to take chances to catch this thing. At least this plan looked feasible.

As he explained it, we would move down the valley one ridge away from the fire. The ridge was extremely steep but only had two patches of timber to obstruct our line. The rest of the ridge was brush and bare ground, ideal for building fire line and burning out. This was our last chance, as farther on the land was covered by big timber and dry as parchment. The winds we had the day before would still be blowing but in our favor. If we could burn off enough before the fire came up the ridge, we would have won.

One division would work off the top burning as they went, while my division would work up from the river. When we tied the lines together, we would spread out to keep our own backfires from jumping the line.

When we reached the river by bus, the same old problem cropped up again. The Spanish-American crews had had their fill with wading the river. They would not cross. Without them the fire plan would not work. I begged them, but it was no use. About that time the line boss arrived in a helicopter. I talked the pilot into ferrying the crews across the river to continue our mission.

Just then the loggers showed up and one of them offered to let us use his boat for future crossings. I called fire camp and told them I had just rented a boat. If that wasn't OK they had better plan on carrying 100 men across the river that evening. This time there were no arguments. Ralph Johnson then called from the district office. He had been put on light duty because of injury. He had heard my conversation and said, laughing, that he had just requisitioned somebody's boat from the office, which would be there by nightfall. We now had a navy.

By the time I had climbed up to meet the crews coming off the top they had initiated their back burns. It had been going great until they ran into the first patch of timber. Their only logger started thinning the trees and in doing so disturbed a yellow jacket nest. The wasps stung his face so badly that his eyes swelled shut. He had to be led off the line. All the other loggers had been sent home and it would take two hours to get another crew. It was already noon and the fire was building up momentum for another run. If it made that run, we couldn't stand it off and would lose our line. We had to chance burning through the timber stand, which would be very risky. I called fire camp and requested permission to make the burn. The answer was no. It was too big a chance to take.

We waited awhile and watched the fire work its way down the opposite hill side. First a patch of timber would explode in fire and a fire ball would roll downhill. The fire would then build up in the brush and with a crack like a rifle shot roar back up the ridge. Soon it would be at the bottom of the ravine and make a run up to our position. Again, we asked permission to burn. The answer was still no.

Al blinked at me. Lives were at stake. We couldn't just sit here helplessly watching the fire burn towards us. We would again be trapped.

I had been told no and if I went against that command it would be my responsibility. Maybe a life might be lost this way as well if we waited any longer. "Let's burn it off," Al said. I nodded, and the men rushed the timber and started hauling every bit of fuel we could lay our hands on across the fire line. Axes and Pulaskis, a combination hoe and axe used in firefighting, were used to trim off all the branches we could reach. Our idea was to burn small strips at a time, thereby lessening the danger of the flames reaching into the treetops and causing a blowup. If the trees blew up our line would be lost. We held our breath, then we could see it was working.

The radio crackled, "Loggers are on their way. When they get there, go through the timber." "Fire camp," I shouted back. "We are already through!" There was silence, then "What? Oh, good."

A few minutes later the fire boss flew over in a copter and lowered a fresh water bag. There was a big grin on his face with a big thumbs up. Our back burn was inching downhill all along our line and now the main fire started to meet it and was struggling for fuel. It looked like our fire was licked.

From that moment on we felt like winners. We began lighting strings of fire that spread out in all directions burning themselves out on the burned-out area. The main fire had stopped its run and was quieting down. A couple days of putting out hot spots and it would be out.

Dusk was falling as we looked across the river. The fire line was black, and the last isolated patches of fuel were blazing away in orange and gold, a beautiful sight against the oncoming darkness. As we worked our way down to the North Fork of the Clearwater, a huge bull elk trotted out of the fire, paused a moment silhouetting his magnificent rack against the skyline, and faded gracefully away.

CHAPTER 9
ARAPAHO NATIONAL FOREST AND SCENIC MANAGEMENT

ANEW CHALLENGE EMERGED on the Arapaho National Forest: How to integrate major visual impacts into the forest landscape? A large mine was proposed in the Williams Fork Drainage in Grand County, Colorado. This was going to cause several impacts to the physical environment and scenic values on the Arapaho and Roosevelt National Forests. It included a major powerline running from Georgetown, Colorado, that would run alongside Interstate 70, parallel to US 40 towards Berthoud Pass, and up over the Continental Divide to the west. There was also a gas line that would run from around Boulder, Colorado, to the west over Rollins Pass above timberline and down into the Grand Valley. These areas were heavily used by the public and adjacent to people's homes. People were outraged, especially in Georgetown. There were many heated meetings between the town and the Public Service Company of Colorado.

Existing powerline cut: This is what we tried to avoid doing

I got a job working with the power company to mitigate the impact of the powerline on the environment as much as possible. It didn't start off well. My old boss on the Fryingpan District of the White River National Forest was now the district ranger on the Clear Creek District of the Arapaho, where the powerline would go. The project engineer for the public service company and this ranger had gotten into a heated argument over a new powerline crossing the Fryingpan District years before. They got reacquainted, and it wasn't friendly; however, this time the engineer knew his job was on the line and he had to give a little. I told him I needed to learn as much as I could about what he could and couldn't do with a project of this size.

I did an evaluation of all the major powerlines in that part of Colorado. With the project engineer we drove and flew all the lines. I was trying to come up with criteria that we could use to evaluate whether a line did scenic or environmental damage, and how much. They were very cooperative. I took a substantial number of photos of what I considered bad and good examples and then evaluated them with the project engineer. It wasn't long before he understood what I was trying to do. Not to prescribe but to look for solutions.

I came up with criteria to judge an alignment, the most important being how visible the powerline would be to the public, including the shape of the vegetation that had to removed and whether the color of the powerline structures and site disturbance to the land had an additional visual impact.

As you drive a highway where do you see a powerline? Right next to the road. The eye is constantly looking at the line rather than the countryside. Sometimes that's the only option but being a national forest, we could vary the location. I wanted to locate the line back away from the highway view and if that was not possible, higher up the slope, so you were not looking right into the structures. In our case the canyon was steep, so we had to move the line up the mountainside. That increased the power company's cost. They were not happy.

I asked them why they couldn't use helicopters to put in the pole structures and to string the line. The ski areas had been using a similar technique to build ski area lifts at both Keystone Ski Area and Copper Mountain. They checked it out and said it might be worth a try. We now could locate pole structures on ridge lines, allowing for easier access for the helicopters and the ability to string line over drainages. Later they were able to pull a lightweight cable between the power pole structures with a helicopter rather than winch the heavy cables from one tower to another. That technique reduced the amount of vegetation that needed to be removed.

I constructed miniature powerline structures that looked like the massive 150-kilovolt or 230-kilovolt powerlines. I then stained them with a variety of colors, including the standard colors the power company used. I took the miniatures to the field, the prairie outside of Golden, Colorado, and to the mountains and took photos of all the options. It turned out the color that was the best at blending into the natural landscape in both prairie and mountain settings was a sage green made by mixing ½ black with ½ yellow colors. Back in the office, I showed the engineers the difference and they agreed. To convince their management, they installed several power poles and stained them the same color as my samples. Our approach was approved. The question was how to achieve the desired color without having to stain poles, a great maintenance cost. We came up with the idea of having the poles treated with copper arsenic, a chemical-based treatment that would give the poles

Test poles to find color that best blended in with the forests

the color we wanted.

That was our solution, at least until the poles finally arrived. I got a call from the project engineer that we had a problem. The poles were a chartreuse color and quite garish. What to do with over a hundred poles. We came up with the idea to sand blast them. Fortunately, that worked, and they were ready for installation.

The use of helicopters also minimized the amount of soil disturbance at the pole locations and reduced the need for access roads. But they said they still needed roads to clear the trees between pole locations, I said, "Why cut the trees when you can pull the cable over them by helicopter?" They said, "We must cut the trees." They said they might interfere with the line. I said, "Just top the trees. We are now at 11,000 feet and higher in

Old and New Powerline Cuts

Next to the highway is an old power line and clearing. Our much larger power-line clearing is on the left, higher up.

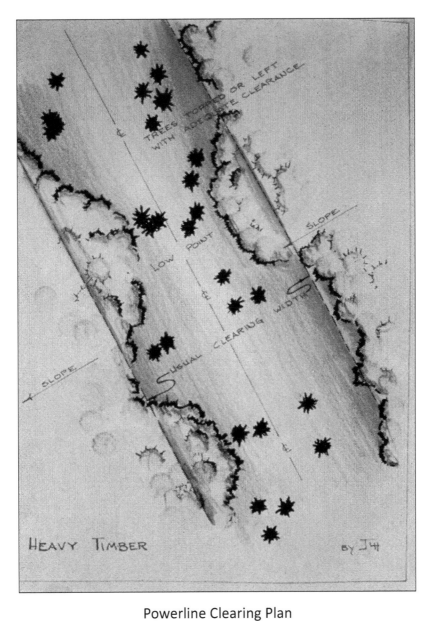

Powerline Clearing Plan

My working drawing for the powerline clearing showing how it could be done without cutting many of the trees.

elevation, close to timberline. A lot of the trees are over one hundred years old. If topped, they will never interfere with the line." They said, "The Forest Service always wants us to cut the trees because of the fire hazard." I said, "What fire hazard?" Well, that got some attention, and we now had the district and forest staffs, including fire staff, meeting on the ground and discussing topping rather than cutting the trees. Was it against policy or just something we had always done? We all agreed we didn't have to cut the trees except the ones next to the poles that could interfere with the powerline.

I did drawings of how I envisioned the right of way clearing would look and briefed the engineers. More importantly, I spent time with the clearing crews going over my drawings and discussing how they could proceed. My past experience working in the woods gave me the confidence to convince the loggers I knew what I was talking about. They all pitched in and did a great job. I now asked the project engineer if we could find a less damaging way of removing the vegetation to be cut than using bulldozers. I had seen horse-logging while I was a smokejumper in Montana and suggested that it might be an option. We sent out the word and found a logger that had two draft horses trained in logging. We tried them out and they were amazing.

Although it was a two-person job, the horses did all the work. One logger would hitch the horse to a log and give it a command. The horse would take the log down the hill to the highway, and the other logger would drop the chain and send the horse back up the hill.

Logging horse at work

The Rollins Pass gas line

The gas line over Rollins Pass offered a different set of problems. Most of the line could be located in existing roads or placed out of sight in the forest. Unfortunately, the line had to cross the pass at an elevation of 11,677 feet, all above timberline in the tundra. The physical damage to this sensitive ecosystem could be substantial. The gas company engineers were committed to trying new construction techniques to mitigate the impacts.

I suggested we move away from the road and down an adjacent draw out of sight. When we flew the route in their helicopter, I noticed a feature that was not natural. From the air this feature was visible but walking on the ground it was hardly noticeable, a pile of rocks about three feet in height. In the air you could see these straight lines running parallel to each other but wider toward the top of the pass and then narrower further down. A definite fan shape. At the time we did not have an

115

Rollins Pass: Olson Game Drive, Rock Wall & Hunting Blind

Aerial View of the Rollins Pass Area

The rock wall and hunting blind on the facing page can be seen in this photo in the lower third of the picture just to the left of center. The apparent trails on the right are parts of a wagon road built by John Quincy Adams Rollins, who found and documented human-made rock structures here in 1873. He wrote of "what, under careful investigation, I conclude are the remains of an ancient settlement. . . stone walls, miles in length, compact and regular and giving every evidence they were created by human hands." The true nature of these structures as game drives is only apparent when viewed from the air. In 1967 and 1969, James Benedict and Byron Olson investigated and documented these game drives.* These two individuals related their findings to the Forest Service in a 1970 report.

Reference:
* "Communal hunting along the Continental Divide of Northern Colorado: Results from the Olson game drive (5BL147), USA." Jason M. LaBelle and Spencer R. Pelton. *Quaternary International* **297** (2013) 45–63. See p. 63.

archeologist working for the Forest Service, so we asked our regional office in Denver to find one to identify this feature. I don't remember who this individual was, but in researching this book I came to believe that the archeologist was James L. Benedict. I found he and a young college student, Byron L. Olson, had jointly written a report for the Forest Service in 1970—not long after my site evaluation in 1967—on the prehistory of Rollins Pass and its man-made features.[1] He said it must have been a prehistoric game trap designed to drive big horn sheep, or other animals, between these stone walls to their death. It was built long before the Native Americans had horses. This ended that route as a possible gas line location as we didn't want to destroy the site. We were now faced with constructing the line across a large expanse of tundra.

We finally came up with a plan that nobody had done before so far as we knew. The pictures on the following pages tell the story better than words.

The line got done and everyone thought we had done a good job. Besides that, we felt like we were a team. I had taken a million pictures and put together a slide talk to explain what we had done. We showed it to the community and both internal and external groups. The public was very complementary, and the Public Service Company of Colorado gave their project engineer a reward, which included taking my slide talk to industry meetings and overseas.

The Washington office saw my slide talk and requested copies for all the Forest Service regions. They also sent me a

1. Benedict, James B., and Olson, Byron L. "Prehistoric Man and Environment in the High Colorado Mountains." Progress Report on field work during the summer of 1969, under National Science Foundation Grant GS–2606. Forest Service report dated 1970.

Digging the Trench for the Gas Line

To dig the trench for the pipeline, old tires were placed on the tundra for the backhoe to drive on. As it moved along, the tires were moved forward.

Saving the Tundra

As we dug the trench, the tundra was carefully removed and set aside, covered and kept damp. The dirt and rocks were put on canvas, avoiding damage to adjacent tundra.

Laying the Cable

Cables were used to winch the steel gas line from one existing road to another. Step by step the pass was crossed. Then, the process was repeated to fill the trench with the removed dirt and replace the tundra.

The Finished Gas Line Job

When done, you needed a trained eye to see the gas line location.
Here, District Ranger Walt Werner is inspecting the finished line.

letter congratulating me on a job well done.

I was invited by several organizations to give my talk. The first was the Colorado Open Space Coordinating Council at the University of Colorado. During questions a lady stood up and raked me and the Forest Service over the coals for doing so much environmental damage. I was a bit taken back and didn't respond. Someone in the audience stood up and defended me, saying, "At least Jim is doing something and not just talking about it." As it turned out, the woman was Estelle Leopold, Aldo Leopold's daughter, representing The Wilderness Society.

Also, after seeing my slide talk the new Regional Forester, William Lucas, brought all his staff out to the forest to see the results of our efforts. During my presentation, the regional fire staff challenged my recommendation to not cut the trees in the right of way. I again repeated what I told the project engineer and said the risks were worth the results.

The Washington office recognized my work in landscape management and recommended to the Public Land Law Review Commission that they might want to interview me. Theodore Edmondson, who was doing a study on powerlines for the commission, came out to the Arapaho National Forest and spent a couple of days with me. We had some great discussions on a variety of subjects.

Through the later part of the sixties I continued working on landscape management projects both from an environmental standpoint and from visual management concerns. I came up with an inventory system to evaluate the land seen from our major highway systems and how relative alteration of the landscape might affect the visual conditions. In later years this approach was adopted by the Washington office, but I am not sure how it was received across all the National Forests.

I enjoyed the variety of projects I got to work on, from powerlines, gas lines, microwave towers and on the new Interstate 70 highway through the Dillon District. Working with the Colorado Highway Department on the interstate project was probably the most challenging, mainly because of their uncompromising attitude. We had some rugged meetings. My goal was to at least improve how this section of interstate fit into the landscape. Since the project also required relocations of major powerlines, my past relationship with Public Service Company of Colorado paid off. They backed my approach and supported my arguments. As our relationship grew they accepted that I was trying to work with them and not against them.

While this work was enjoyable and challenging, my real love was ski area development. While I had the basic skills as a landscape architect, I started out knowing nothing about ski areas. In fact, I didn't even know how to ski. As I mentioned earlier, I put all my personal time into learning how to ski and how ski areas are built and managed. I traveled to most of the Western United States visiting ski areas and talking to the Forest Service rangers and ski area managers.

This paid off. I was able to convince Chuck Lewis at Copper Mountain Ski Area to paint his ski lifts so they would blend in with the natural setting. He used the same color that I had developed for the powerline project, a sage green. It really helped to blend the lifts into the surrounding vegetation. Soon after that, Keystone adopted the same color scheme.

Now, after about ten years, I could be totally involved in Forest Service potential ski area inventories and on-site development. I organized district teams to do assessments of all the potential mountains in Northern Colorado and did a report outlining the mountains that had merit and those that did not. This wasn't just an office job, as I was able to climb or snowcat to most of these mountains and do an assessment of their base area development potential.

I had planned a trip to Europe to attend the 1968 Winter Olympics in Grenoble, France, with my friend Don Campbell and suddenly got sick. It was sort of like mononucleosis. No energy, a low-grade fever, and other symptoms. This all started after New Year's Eve, 1968. I went to the hospital for a week but got no results. I took a trip to my sister Miriam's home in California to rest, but that didn't help. I was having trouble caring for myself and finally in desperation returned to my parents' home in Burlington, Iowa. There I sat for two months until I started to feel better and returned to my job at the Arapaho National Forest.

Shortly after I returned to work, Forest Supervisor Wally Lloyd rewarded me with a step increase in wages for my landscape architecture and visual management work on the Arapaho National Forest. At that time, my proudest achievement.

Land Planning

Soon afterwards, Wally moved to Region 3 in New Mexico and a new forest supervisor was named, Don Biddison. Don came from the Washington office but had spent most of his field time in California. He was a modest man and excellent boss. He had a passion for moving the Forest Service forward in project-level planning. We had a number of discussions, and I offered to explore how we could improve. That's how I got involved in what they now called "ecosystem management." I took the concepts that were being advocated by a planner and landscape architect in Minnesota by the name of Ian McHarg. In his book *Designing with Nature*, Ian advocated using a series of overlays of diverse types of ecological information to show opportunities

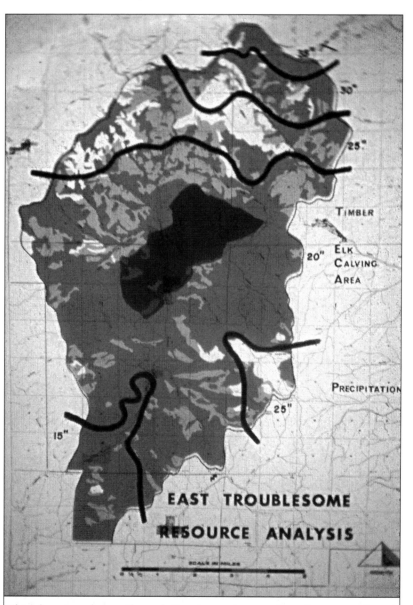

This drawing shows the relative importance of environmental and resource considerations in the area: The darker the color, the more issues there are that need to be resolved.

and potential problems. His work was focused on urban or regional planning but applied just as well to large areas of national forest lands. It was simple, but radical in the planning world at that time. Ian was noted for being one of the fathers of the concepts of geographic information systems and ecosystem planning and management.

The first project area we tackled was an area called East Troublesome. It was one of the last areas on the forest that had a potential supply of timber but was roadless in character. I applied the overlay concept to this area and broke it down into ecological units with different capabilities. What the analysis showed was that the road into the area would cause significant soil damage and environmental problems. There was concern about my analysis, so Don took several of us on a hike and camping trip throughout the area. After verifying the analysis was correct, Don said, "We're not going to enter the area." This was a blow to the National Forest's timber management pro-gram, as the Arapaho National Forest had already overcut the country that had roads and had nowhere else to go. As a land-scape architect, I had no problem with cutting trees for whatever purpose. However, I did have a problem with building roads into every high-country valley. In Colorado, at that time, even the ranchers were becoming upset with the Forest Service's road building policies.

CHAPTER 10

AVALANCHE

A near death experience

U P UNTIL NOW, I have not talked about my social life. I was now thirty-two years old and living in Denver, Colorado. I had several professional friends who were all single and we were having a blast. I still spent most of my time in the mountains skiing, hiking, and hunting but also belonged to a tennis club and socialized in the Denver party scene.

On Memorial Day 1969 a bunch of my friends organized a trip to Taos, New Mexico, to ski, whitewater raft, and play tennis. We arrived on a Friday evening and gathered at a Mexican restaurant.

Across from me was this girl. She said, "Aren't you the guy that tried to pick me up in Vail, Colorado, a couple of years ago?" I did not recognize her, but as we talked I remembered that I saw a girl at Vail who I thought I had dated at Iowa State University. I went up to her and said, "Did you go to Iowa State?" She said, "Yes." I said, "Were you a Chi Omega?" She said "Yes." I said, "I think I dated you." She said, "No, you didn't." That was the end of the conversation.

It turns out the girl was Gretchen Gantert, my future wife. We started dating shortly after that trip and we were together all summer and fall of 1969.

Come the holiday season, Gretchen returned home to Dubuque, Iowa, to visit her parents. I arranged to go to Glenwood Springs, Colorado, to go hunting with my good friend Bob Veltus.

On Christmas Eve, there was a huge storm brewing in the Northern Rockies from Montana to Colorado. Several feet of snow fell that night. Up to four feet of snow fell at Breckenridge, Colorado. When I heard about the weather, I was up early, off to Breckenridge Ski Area and powder skiing. I planned to ski until early afternoon then head for Glenwood.

The following is taken from a letter I wrote to the forest supervisor of the Arapaho National Forest on January 6, 1970, of the events that happened that day.

Dick Shafer, the snow ranger on the Dillon District, was out on avalanche control at the Breckenridge Ski Area. I had earlier said I would ski with him but was unable to contact him when I got to the ski area. I skied powder by myself until around 12:45 P.M. I then ran into Dick and he asked me if I would like to accompany him and two area ski patrolmen to look at a recent slide path in an adjacent bowl on Peak 8. I agreed. The bowl was around one-mile wide and a couple of thousand feet high, from top to bottom. Average slope was probably around sixty percent plus, extremely steep, and all of it avalanche hazard. Earlier in the morning the patrol had placed two charges of explosives in the area and a fracture line the entire width of the bowl had released a slide. The fracture line varied from four feet to seven feet high. The reason for us going out on the slope to look at that fracture line was not quite clear to me. It seemed they wanted to look at the various snow layers and on which layer the slide had been triggered.

Everyone put on their orange nylon avalanche cords except me. I had left mine in the car. We traversed out onto the slide area directly below the four-foot fracture line. In digging down into the snow there was about three feet of crust and depth hoar, an almost ice-like substance, remaining in the slide area below the fracture line. I mentioned to Dick that it appeared very unstable. Dick reassured me that it had to be stable with that much shooting and the size of the slide. I was apprehensive about staying out there, especially since I didn't have my avalanche cord.

The rest of the group had moved out away from me and we were all about fifty feet apart, with the patrolman Rick in the lead. Al was next, then Dick. I thought I should go back and turned to look for a safe way out. I heard a sharp loud sound, like a clap of thunder. My first reaction was that a charge had gone off but as I looked up the slope I could see a new fracture line going across the top of the slope and the snow starting to move.

Since the big load of snow was still above us there was not an immediate movement of snow under my skis. I turned my skis downhill into a schuss thinking I could reach a rock outcropping and possibly out-ski the slide. I thought I was the only one caught in the slide.

I skied perhaps a second or two when the major impact of snow hit me and took my breath away. For some reason when I started to move with the slide I could breathe much easier. I thought that since I didn't have an avalanche cord it was up to me to save myself. My right leg was being bent behind me by the pressure on my ski when the binding finally released. I had Arlberg straps on, which fixed my skis to my body and while the skis had released they were swinging around and gave me some good belts.

The sensation of speed was fantastic. I was now riding in a sea of snow going ever faster. The ride was very rough, and I was being tossed around. It was like being in a flume of water, where I was occasionally able to catch a breath of air. Initially I couldn't tell which way was up, but I was finally able to ori-entate myself. I worked my way into a sitting position, with my feet downhill, and tried to swim as if I was treading water. That seemed to work, and I instantly started to rise in the snow. I kept doing this as I sped downhill and increased the swimming motion as the slide slowed down. The slide decreased in speed slowly.

I swam until I could feel the slide begin to stop. I was still buried at the time, how deep I didn't know, but it seemed deep. I pulled my hands to my face to give me some breathing room and at that moment the slide came to a rather abrupt stop. I thrust my hands forward and I found my head and hands free from the snow. The slide was still moving very slightly, and I worked my body out until I was sitting on the surface. I pulled my feet out and released my Arlberg straps.

My first reaction was that I was the only one caught. I looked uphill and saw the entire hill had slide but Rick the patrolman was standing on the edge of the slide. I yelled at him to ask if anyone else was caught and he yelled back that both Al and Dick were in the slide. I heard shouts and ran over to find Dick. He was OK but still partly buried. Looking uphill I spotted a small piece of orange cord protruding from the snow. I ran to the cord and yelled at Rick to go for help, that I had found where Al was buried.

I used the cord to pull myself up the slope until it pointed straight down. I made one swipe with my hand uphill from the cord knowing that the cord was tied to his waist. On the second swipe I hit an object and I was able to dig out Al's head, it was about fourteen inches below the surface. I cleaned out his mouth and he started to breathe. As I continued digging Dick arrived; he seemed to be OK but complained of his knee hurting. As it turned out he had a slight fracture of the lower leg. By this time the snow had set up like concrete and we had to use our bare hands to dig Al out. It wasn't until members of the rescue team arrived with shovels that we finally got him out.

At that time, I glanced at my watch. It was now 1:25 P.M. The slide had occurred at about 1:15. It had taken me about five to seven minutes to get out of the slide and to find Al and free his head. It was twenty minutes later that the rescue party arrived.

Now, I was able to glance at the slide and make an estimate of the size. From the original fracture line, the snow above it for about 100 to 200 feet had slid. It appeared that fracture line had gone all the way to the top of the ridge, but it was actually a curved shape about 300 feet wide. The fracture line appeared to be about four feet deep and possibly higher. The area we were in when the slide hit us was now exposed, bare earth. My estimate of the distance the slide carried was from 1,000 feet to 2,000 feet down a sixty percent slope.

It wasn't until the rescue party arrived that I got a little worried about the remaining snow hanging above us. It appeared the rescue party was going to go out on an area that hadn't slid. We yelled for them to wait. They immediately stopped and waited while a small party took a safer route with the toboggan and more shovels. Al's feet were buried about four feet under the snow and it took a lot of effort to finally free him.

The patrolman on the hill kept yelling at us to get out of there and later asked why we didn't. The reason was that Dick's leg was hurting him and he felt he could get out easier on skis rather than trying to walk in deep snow. But first we had to retrieve one of his skis that was buried.

I started out first and met the snowcat that was coming to pick up Dick and Al. They had injuries including broken bones and muscle spasms. Al had gone into shock. I was OK but later in the evening felt like I had played football all day.

Only recently, while attempting to find my letter for my children, I came upon a document published by Knox Williams, who was an avalanche expert for the U.S. Forest Service Research Station in Fort Collins, Colorado. Knox published a summary of avalanche accident reports to help those who spend time in the mountains in the winter to avoid getting caught in an avalanche, or if caught how to survive. He had found my letter in an article in The Denver Post and included it in his report. He pointed out that because Dick and I were swimming, it was a major factor in our survival. The most important thought was that Al Brit's avalanche cord is the first documented case of a victim being saved by using one. Fortunately, the beacons used now provide more protection, but the only true protection is to avoid avalanche areas when there are adverse conditions.

Years later a friend, Carl Gidlund, called me. He asked if I had read the recent Reader's Digest. I said no. He said there was an article summarizing a book written by McKay Jenkins called *The White Death* about an avalanche on Mt. Cleveland in Glacier National Park, Montana, that killed five young men from the University of Montana on the same day I was caught in Colorado. In the book, the author quoted my write-up.

Looking back, we can be thankful we survived. It was an awful incident and one which we could have avoided with a little common sense. We were all experienced in skiing and avalanches, but you can't second-guess Mother Nature.

After a debriefing at the Breckenridge Ski Area base lodge with the area management and the county sheriff, I headed for Glenwood Springs, Colorado, and Bob's house. He answered the door with a hearty Merry Christmas, and I said, "Yes, and I need a stiff drink."

As I said in my report, "In conclusion, I might say that it was the best Christmas gift I have ever had in my life, to end up sitting on top of that slide."

CHAPTER 11

CHANGING COURSE

My new wife Gretchen, best man Don Campbell, with the hat,
and I in the Mount of the Holy Cross Wilderness, Colorado

M Y WEEK HUNTING with Bob Veltus was filled with uncertainty. How could I go on like this? I was now thirty-three years old, and while I was enjoying my work, I couldn't see a future. I seemed to go from one girl to another and was never satisfied. Now I had met a wonderful girl that I loved, but would it be another breakup?

That New Year's Eve, Gretchen and I went to the Vail, Colorado, home of my friends Don and Carol Campbell for a party, and I proposed to her. She said yes.

Our Honeymoon

My life changed course again. We decided to get married early in the spring. Gretchen's break from teaching was at Easter. She wanted to go someplace warm for our honeymoon. I went to a travel agent and reserved a hotel in Cozumel, Mexico. I had friends who had gone there and said it was an unknown paradise. The week before our wedding our travel agent called to say we had a change of plans. Our hotel canceled all but two nights, but a Mexican travel agent had made reservations at two different resorts in Merida, Mexico, and Chichen Itza, a Mexican tourist attraction, but without transportation between resorts. Our honeymoon turned into a nightmare.

We left Denver shortly after the wedding and flew to New Orleans to stay overnight before we flew to Merida, Mexico. We were exhausted and while calling a cab to take us to the hotel, I left my plane tickets in the airport. I spent the next morning straightening that out and we finally boarded a plane to Mexico. Upon arriving I told the attendant where we were staying. No one had heard of it. Finally, a cab driver said he might know so we got into his cab and he drove out of the airport and then

New Year's Eve Party Invitation

This is a photograph of the original invitation to the party during which I proposed to Gretchen—and she said, "Yes."

turned into a construction site. It was a new resort, which had been under construction, and this was its opening night.

They treated us like royalty. They put us in a villa in the center of the complex and said dinner was at eight. We went to dinner, and we were the only guests. We had three waiters and musicians serenading us. After dinner, we went to the bar to dance to a swinging band with no one else there. It was a fun time but creepy.

The next day they took us on a tour to Uxmal, ruins of the Mayan civilization. While Gretchen waited at the bottom of a pyramid, I climbed to the top. Quite steep, with narrow stairs. While there, I heard someone crying. On a narrow bench was an American teacher in total panic. She had climbed up the pyramid and now could not climb down the steep decline. It took me an hour to get her back down with a cable. Gretchen said, "Where have you been?"

We had to leave Merida for Cozumel, an island off the southern coast of the Yucatan peninsula. Our only transportation was a bus leaving at 5:30 A.M. We were the only Americans. The bus was crowded, with chickens riding on top. We got very hungry as the day passed, but at our stops the only things to eat were tacos in washtubs covered with flies. We finally arrived at our ferry where another American couple gave us half a loaf of bread. We were overjoyed to board the ferry. We were on the lower deck with plenty of room to spare. Then hordes of people arrived. Soon it was standing room only and the boat was overloaded.

As we headed out to sea, the boat kept close to shore. Gretchen said, "What are they doing?" I said, "I think there are heavy seas and they are trying to go to the island in the shortest distance." I was right. Now the waves were coming over the sides and we were wet to our waists. People were getting sick.

It was not a good situation. I told Gretchen if this boat goes over swim as hard as you can away from the boat. I'll be beside you. We finally made it to shore and got to our lovely hotel, totally worn out.

I spent the next couple of days trying to figure out how we were going to get off this island when our room was no longer available. I did a little snorkeling and Gretchen laid out in the sun. I forgot to mention that earlier in the winter we went skiing and Gretchen broke her ankle. She had gotten the cast off before our wedding. She was not out in the sun long before she had a second-degree burn on her ankle.

I finally got a plane ticket back to Merida. At Merida I talked a cab driver into driving us to Chichen Itza. It was against his company's policy but for fifty American dollars he said, "¡Si!" The hotel at Chichen Itza was brand new and fabulous. We lined up a guide to take us through the Mayan ruins the next day. The guide had worked for the explorer who had found and uncovered the ruins. A very knowledgeable fellow. He said, "We must leave very early." We were at the main pyramid when it opened and the first ones to enter the interior passage that climbed to the top. At the top was a stone jaguar with green emerald eyes. Our guide said we must go out now. As we headed down, the passage had already started to heat up. It was only a few feet wide and difficult for two people passing each other. Tour groups were already coming up the steep stairs sweating heavily. Years later I heard that they closed this passage because of serious injuries to tourists. I can see why.

After all we went through, I was ready to go back to Colorado. We returned to Merida then flew to Miami, Florida. Great to be back in the USA. We returned to Denver and moved into our rented duplex and settled back into our jobs.

Lake Tahoe

That summer the forest supervisor got a call from the regional office with a request for me to go to Lake Tahoe in California and Nevada to work on a team doing a recreation plan for both Regions 4 and 5, which co-managed the Tahoe Basin. The Washington office was coordinating the effort. I was the only landscape architect on the team of foresters. There were five of us altogether along with a support staff for clerical work. I had only been married a few months and was reluctant to say yes, but Gretchen had a full-time job and she thought a job with this much exposure would help my career.

It was a terrific opportunity. The team had very little idea on how to proceed. The Washington office representative had an inventory system he wanted used to identify the recreation opportunities throughout the basin. It is ironic that the concept was the same as Arthur Carhart had advocated for in 1922 to be used on the San Isabel National Forest in Colorado.

We started with the inventory. The parameters were identifying the physical attributes of the land and the possible negative aspects of human use. I reached back into my old land use planning training from college and suggested that we use the same principles as city planning for our planning process and identify different management zones like a city plan. The team liked that idea.

Our first step was to do the inventory of recreation opportunities. The second was to allocate recreation use options to unique areas of the forest based on their potential and public demands. The third step was to construct rules on how these areas could be managed to maintain or enhance their potential for recreation. I did a mockup of a portion of the basin and we presented the concept to the various forest managers. They bought into the concept and we worked for the next couple months determining the best option for each management area and completing the plan for the manager's approval.

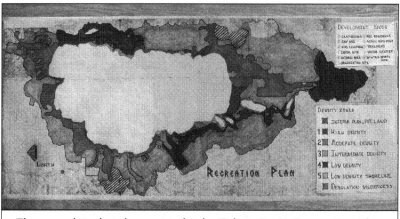

The completed and approved Lake Tahoe Basin Recreation Plan

One problem emerged. While the management areas fell into place, the transportation system around the lake bisected the areas. The managers wanted a tool to evaluate the areas that needed to be protected with zoning requirements and the areas that already had serious detrimental effects on the visual aspects with recommendations on how these road corridors could be improved. I gladly took on the problem, as I had already completed a visual management analysis for the Arapaho National Forest and that concept fit right into what they wanted. I worked with the research scientists at the Forest Service Research Station in Berkley, California. We took a simple weighted evaluation process and updated it to judge each section of highway on different attributes. When this was done it showed where areas should be protected from undesirable development and areas where investments should be made to improve the existing situation.

I'm not sure where this all went after I left for Colorado, but I used the concept we came up with as both a district ranger and regional planner later in my career.

Gretchen came come out to visit and we spent a long weekend in San Francisco and took in some shows at Lake Tahoe. She now had a sense of my job and career options and saw that I didn't have much of a career with the Forest Service. I was now a GS-11 at 33 years of age and the only position above me was a GS-12 at the regional level and that position was filled by a young man.

I Quit, Then I'm a District Ranger

After Gretchen left for Denver, I thought long and hard and had to agree with her. I loved my work and the people, but to sit in that job for twenty-five more years would be discouraging. I had been approached by a design firm in Denver that specialized in ski areas. They had offered me a job, as they needed someone with my ski area design background. I called them, and we came to tentative agreement on the job. I then called my boss Chuck McConnell, who had moved to the Arapaho National Forest a year earlier and broke the news to him that I would be leaving the organization.

Just before I returned home I got a call from Don Biddison, the forest supervisor, saying that he would like to offer me the district ranger job in Dillon, Colorado. I was floored. A landscape architect being named a district ranger was unheard of, especially a promotion to one of the premier districts in Region 2. I called Gretchen with the news and told her this was a great honor and I thought I had enough experience to do the job. I knew it was going to be tough, as the Forest Service did not have a good reputation in Summit County. The reaction in the

Forest Service community was also shock. At least two people appealed the decision.

Less than a year from my avalanche accident and almost losing my life, my world turned upside down. I got married and became a forester. My career took a hard turn in a different direction.

CHAPTER 12

MY LANDSCAPE ARCHITECTURE CAREER

My real love was working on ski area development

I averaged sixty days a year of both work and personal time learning the skills necessary to provide leadership for this important Forest Service program.

WHEN I ACCEPTED the job as district ranger, my career as a landscape architect in the Forest Service ended. While the landscape architecture skills in my future positions were not officially used, much of what I had learned on the job and in college was a great benefit to me as a forester.

To most people a landscape architect primarily does designs of outdoor spaces for personal residences, businesses and city parks. My career was totally different, with a few exceptions. This chapter summarizes the work that I accomplished as a landscape architect. It was taken from a statement of achievement that was composed by my former boss, Chuck McConnell.

I always felt I owed Chuck for my job with the Forest Service. He was a natural mentor and challenged me to be innovative. He first hired me as a crew leader then supported me for my first permanent job as a landscape architect. His encouragement gave me the opportunity to try different tasks, many of which had nothing to do with my profession but broadened my understanding of the Forest Service organization and how it operated. He encouraged and supported me to move to a district office as an assistant. He ended up as my supervisor on the Arapaho National Forest in Golden, Colorado, before I was promoted to the Dillon District ranger position. This writeup was done a year prior to that move. It was done in governmental format.

I have rearranged it so that it makes more sense as a story.

STATEMENT OF ACHIEVEMENT

Mr. Hagemeier has exceptional insight into the value and potential uses of recreation sites and their relationship to the total land use and environmental picture. His evaluation of proposed development sites always included well thought-out perceptions of the sites' reaction to diverse types of use, including their ability to withstand human use and whether each site is desirable or undesirable from a management viewpoint. In many cases his recommendations indicate that no development should be made of a given site or area because the adverse effect of such developments would, in the future, be far greater than any immediate benefits.

From my personal knowledge I know of his proposal to remove the road from the shoreline of Maroon Lake while redesigning the campground. Maroon Lake is on the White River National Forest and a gateway to the Maroon Bells Wilderness Area. Jim's well thought out arguments sold the concept to the district ranger and forest supervisor over the objections of the forest lands and engineering staffs. That decision changed the entire character and attractiveness of this world-class scenic area.

A few years later he was assigned the task of designing a new road and resort on Trappers Lake, which at that time sat next to the Flat Top Primitive Area. His evaluation recommended against this proposal and offered an alternative location for a road and campground away from the lakeshore. He again argued that Trappers Lake was too special and should be protected in its natural state. As a result, Trappers Lake still qualified to be included in the new Wilderness Area years later.

Perhaps the best example is his re-evaluation of the proposed development plan for Dillon Reservoir. In this case he quickly realized that the plan would soon turn the area into a recreational slum. His new concept was to keep sites small with connecting access roads, providing a more natural and private camping experience. It allowed management to open and close sites as use dictated, saving time and money. This helped to preserve the unique environmental surroundings and balance the recreation development with the carrying capacity of the reservoir and its visual quality. A somewhat radical idea for this region in 1968.

It had been years since the Arapaho National Forest has had the funds for new construction. About the time Jim arrived thousands of dollars became available. To accomplish all the planning, design and construction review was his major workload for several years. Jim's plans for Forest Service improvements are constantly above average in their concept and utility. He has a keen knowledge of flow patterns and space utilization. His plans and thoughtful advice for development reflect his experience at the ranger district level, as both a smokejumper and a highly qualified fire specialist. One has only to spend time using these sites to see they are some of the best in Region Two of the Forest Service. Forest visitors often comment on how well done and pleasant they are.

As time went by and recreation dollars decreased, Jim became an invaluable assistant to the forest supervisor and district rangers in specific technical solutions in all functional activities concerning their relationship to landscape management. The Arapaho National Forest sits next to the Denver metropolitan area with major highways bisecting the forest. Thousands of visitors and locals drive through or live in the forest. The values the forest offered were very important to the public and they became quick to respond if they thought they were being damaged. He developed a concept of identifying "seen areas" as viewed from the roads with criteria on blending development into the visual corridor. He used this concept to train district personnel on how to mitigate the adverse visual effects from manmade intrusions such as timber sales, powerlines, etc. Because of these efforts this summer the

Arapaho National Forest was selected as a study area for the new "multiple use planning approach" based on the chief's "forest land stratification study." Jim, more than anyone else, is responsible for the forest employees' attitude and respect toward the forest landscape environment.

In the fall of 1968 a large mining operation was proposed by Climax Molybdenum Company in the Williams Fork River. The proposal called for a major powerline to run from Georgetown, Colorado along Interstate 70 and Highway 40. In addition, a gas line was proposed to run from Boulder, Colorado, over [Rollins] Pass, into the Grand Valley to the west. Both projects would have significant impacts to the forest environment. The public and all the environment groups were very upset. Jim was assigned the task of liaison between Public Service Company of Colorado for the powerline and Western Slope Gas Company for the gas line. His job was to work with the companies on mitigating the environmental impacts as much as possible.

Working closely with the companies, Jim completely revised the way they located, cleared and constructed the powerline. He convinced the company of his methods and worked with the construction crews, so they understood his recommendations. The results were stunning. As a result, Public Service Company revised the way they build all their powerlines. Jim then put together a slide talk showing what they wanted to accomplish and the results after construction was finished. That talk got wide distribution in the Forest Service and with the nation's power companies. Jim personally went to dozens of meetings presenting his talk from South Dakota to New Mexico. He was also well received by the Colorado Open Space Coordinating Council, ([which was] normally highly critical of development).

His work on these projects led to his being assigned to work with the Colorado Highway Department on the extension of Interstate 70 through the Blue River Valley to Vail Pass. This became a challenging task, as they had not been cooperative in trying to mitigate environmental impacts through the forest. Since powerlines needed to be relocated, his relationship with Public Service Company of Colorado helped convince the Highway Department to listen to Jim's suggestions. Jim conceived and sold the idea that this section of highway should be the most beautiful and well-designed of the entire system, if possible. The power companies pitched in, including the Bureau of Reclamation, and adopted the same techniques used on their powerline next to Georgetown, Colorado. The highway engineers also began brainstorming ideas, with the results being splitting the interstate lanes, stream improvements and building a bike path along the highway. Ideas way beyond their time. (These ideas were adopted, and Interstate Highway 70 from Silverthorne, Colorado, to Glenwood Springs, Colorado, is one of the most environmentally compatible sections in the country.) The National Forest Office in Washington recognized Jim's efforts in dealing with outside industry and recommended that the Public Lands Law Review Commission review his work. They sent Theodore Edmondson, who was doing a study on powerline impacts for the commission, to interview Jim.

While Jim has had many successes working with all types of industrial impacts to National Forest lands, his personal interest was in winter sports, particularly ski area development. Jim has achieved his expertise in winter sports planning and ski area layout almost entirely on his own. He spent a great deal of personal time and money traveling to most of the winter sports areas in the West. He made contacts with Forest Service administrators of those areas and formulated his own ideas of the problems and workable solutions to solve them. His ideas in planning and design of ski areas has caught the eye of area managers. As a result, he is well respected by the Ski Area Managers Association, Tell Ertl of Lake Eldora, Harry Baum of Breckenridge, and others. Since planning for ski areas is in its beginning stages, professional planners have sought out advice from Jim. His ideas have helped . . . the Forest Service ensure that winter sports areas fit into the total environment rather than determine the environment.

With the rapid growth of skiing in Colorado, the National Forest lands have become besieged with applications for new areas along with the community and associated development. In this area, Jim excels the most. In 1969 he helped develop a program to inventory the skiing potential on the entire Arapaho National Forest looking at all the proposed areas and any other mountain that might have potential for a new area. He helped organize teams from the ranger districts and supervisor's office balancing various disciplines and technical experience, resulting in a well-rounded evaluation. He wrote a report that summarized the findings of these teams, which made recommendations for permits for Keystone and Copper Mountain ski areas and rationale for denying permits on other proposals. The Washington office, because of a recreation audit of Region Two, instructed the regional forester to make a similar regionwide inventory of winter sports sites.

From my viewpoint, I feel that much of the Arapaho National Forest's success in developing an outstanding recreation program and in avoiding serious environmental problems caused both from outside and service induced impacts can be attributed to the sound recommendations of Jim

Hagemeier. Not only has he done his job well but in such a manner that a wide range of people, both in private industry and the Forest Service, have benefitted from his expertise in landscape management. For this reason, I recommend Jim be given a special achievement award for sustained performance; with a financial reward.

    Charles E. McConnell
    Staff Officer
    Recreation & Lands
    Arapaho National Forest

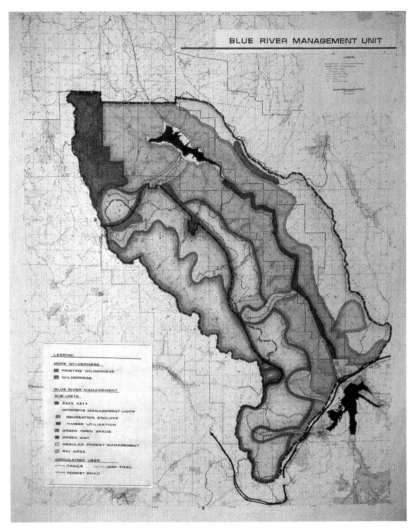

The Blue River Management Plan

This is the plan I developed for the extension of Interstate 70 through the Blue River Valley to Vail Pass. The planned route of I-70 is shown by the black line near the bottom of the picture.

CHAPTER 13

SUMMIT COUNTY, COLORADO

Our home at the Dillon ranger station,
looking into the Gore–Eagles Nest Wilderness Area

I HAD BARELY BEEN named the new district ranger in Summit County, Colorado, when we were invited to a welcoming party at David and Susan Ray's ranch. I had earlier worked with David on his proposed ski area and Gretchen and I had become friends with the Rays. They had over hundred people there including all the community leaders and the Summit County Commissioners. It was a great start for us. Also included was Larry Steenrod. Larry and I were great friends from Denver, and he was in our wedding party. He had a cabin in Breckenridge, Colorado, and had recently moved to the county to open an insurance business. Everyone in Breckenridge knew and liked Larry, and he was a great help introducing us around.

Summit County was humming with development and constant proposals for more. In addition, the state of Colorado was in the planning stage for Interstate 70, running from Silverthorne to Vail Pass. The Eisenhower Tunnel under the Continental Divide was two years away from completion. When finished, it would flood the county with more visitors. In anticipation, the new Keystone Ski Area and village was under construction, Breckenridge Ski area was expanding, and Copper Mountain Ski Area and village were getting ready to start construction. These developments impacted national forest lands and much of the private lands in the Blue River Valley.

It was critical that all the governments work together. That was my top priority. This was not easy. Lee Woolsey, Summit County's manager, must have had an unpleasant experience with the Forest Service. For some time, he would not return my calls. However, we became good friends.

My second priority was to foster land use planning in the county. Virtually every private development impacted national forest lands. Constant trespass on public lands from roads, cabins, and other structures was a problem.

My third priority was to improve management of the district, especially being as efficient as possible within a limited budget. My district had one of the largest recreation workloads in the region and was being heavily impacted by ski area development on national forest lands.

My last priority was to persuade the Colorado State Highway Department to change the way they constructed Interstate 70, which ran west from Denver. The Straight Creek section on the Dillon District of the Forest Service, which runs from the Eisenhower Tunnel to Silverthorne, Colorado, was an environmental disaster. Without listening to the geologists, the highway department had undercut unstable soils to the point that the entire mountainside was sliding into the stream below.

Starting with relationships, I volunteered to be on the county planning board. This was virtually unheard of for the Forest Service at that time. I had to get permission from the forest supervisor and regional office. It helped, as I could sit down with Lee Woolsey and get briefed on all the various development proposals, then review their impacts on national forest lands. At the county planning meetings, I could then question the developers on whether they had applied to the Forest Service to allow a permitted use. I could also provide the board information on the development from a professional planner's perspective. This relationship grew stronger as it became apparent that both the county and the Forest Service were benefiting. When the developer went before the county commissioners for approval, we had a unified approach on what needed to be done to improve the proposal or reject it.

It became apparent that the county needed to update their planning and zoning requirements. One of the individuals I had become acquainted with was Bob Arceri. Bob was a partner in a local planning firm. He was a landscape architect who had graduated from Iowa State University. His firm also had a couple of architects on their staff. Bob shared my concerns about the county planning regulations, and he and I volunteered to rewrite them.

This may seem like it was beyond my responsibility, but I looked at it another way. If we found a trespass road, building, or any development on public land, the Forest Service's only recourse was to site the trespassers with a federal charge. The result was either a long, drawn out process or the judge didn't want to bother with it and the Forest Service was forced into allowing the trespass (or free use of public lands for private profit). In writing the regulations I wrote them to require the developer to review their possible impacts to all land, be it Forest Service or county property. If the developer failed to do the evaluation it would be a county violation. This way the sheriff could write a citation and it was immediately acted on by the county judge.

The county and Forest Service partnered to promote a land planning exercise to improve the county's land use zoning. We had public sessions at Keystone Ski Area to define what we thought would happen, what we wanted to prevent, and what we wanted to happen. We had some lively discussions. We incorporated the results into maps of the county, showing where those issues applied. This visual information gave the public an idea where the problems were and how the revised zoning would help. The effort was a great success.

One day, the county surveyor called to say he wanted to show me something. I met him in Breckenridge and we drove to a new condo development. The developer had placed the building right on the edge of national forest land. One of the decks hung over the line and a gentleman was on the deck sipping his cocktail. We decided to have some fun. The surveyor, in a loud voice, directed me to tie flags on the trees and climb up and tie flags on the deck. In shock, the fellow asked what I was doing, and I explained to him the deck was trespassing on public land. Weeks later as I was driving by the condo I looked up to see the deck had been sawed in half with the trespass portion removed. Maybe our efforts were paying off.

The ski areas were a huge impact. I was coordinating with the areas and the county on their village plans as well as all their development on the mountain. Years earlier Breckenridge Ski Area had bulldozed ski runs down the mountain, creating huge wash outs and environmental damage. We were determined not to let that happen again in the rush to build the new areas. I was fortunate to get a new assistant ranger by the name of Pat Lynch. Pat was one of the best helpers I ever had in the Forest Service. I put him in charge of managing the ski area mountain development and he did an outstanding job. He developed a checklist the areas had to follow before they could do any construction. The only problem I had was that I didn't have enough money to support all the time he needed. I went to the area managers and said if they could each put up $3,000 we could then afford to have Pat on their projects full time. Chuck Lewis, the manager of Copper Mountain, immediately sent the money. However, Clay Simon, the Keystone manager, was reluctant. He asked me for a letter to explain to Keystone's owners my rationale. I typed up a letter but then I decided not to give it to him as I knew this was against Forest Service policy (though unwritten) to ask for money from a developer. Somehow, he got an unsigned copy. The next thing I know I got a call from the forest supervisor who said the regional forester had called him and the Washington office of the Forest Service was very upset with me. As I found out, Clay had taken the unsigned letter to Washington and Congress and said they needed to help finance the district to do this job. The annual budget from Congress authorized $9,000 additional dollars to the Dillon District for summer work on ski area construction. I pleaded innocent.

We had several disagreements with the ski areas, but most were easily solved, except for Keystone. Clay was under pressure to reduce his costs and some of the issues were difficult to solve. However, his wife and Gretchen had become good friends, so we still socialized together.

I did have one regret with Keystone. Upstream from the area in Montezuma Basin, a mining company had the area covered with mining claims. The claims owner was now trying to take the area to patent and he would then be the owner of national forest land. The area had a low grade of iron oxide that was not valuable. We tried to stop this from happening and after several years and court cases we finally won, but I dropped the ball. I was so tied up with that case I didn't pursue attempting to remove the stream next to Keystone from mineral entry. As a result, years later, someone claimed the land next to the village under the 1872 Mining Act and it caused financial hardships for Keystone.

One good thing happened as a result of the publicity on the mining claim issue. A TV station in Denver came up to the district and did a couple of interviews with me about the mining claims. I developed a good relationship with the reporter and we agreed to do a weekly TV spot on Forest Service activities on the district. It was a fantastic opportunity for me to talk about some of the recreation issues, such as trespass fires and trash cleanup, but also an update on construction activities around the county on Forest Service lands. It gave the Forest Service some weekly exposure in the Denver metro area.

One day I was driving down Ten Mile Creek between Frisco and Copper Mountain Ski Area when I saw four-wheel-drive vehicles driving in the middle of the creek. They were a crew filming a commercial for Jeep. I was furious and ended up kicking them off the district and writing them a ticket. They just laughed me off and said they would pay the fine and that would be that. I was telling my TV friend about the incident and he suggested I confiscate the film, since it had been taken illegally. I contacted our law enforcement people in Denver and they arranged for another agency to confiscate the film from the company's office. That made our day and cost them a lot more than a fifty-dollar ticket.

The district recreation program had developed into a giant workload. On weekends the people were lined up on the highway trying to get into the campgrounds around Dillon Reservoir. We had a capacity for 5,000 people. When I arrived, the staff had been trying various things to make ends meet. The most innovative was using three-wheeled bicycles rather than pickups to clean campgrounds. That way we could station employees at the campgrounds and reduce the cost of several rental pickups. The Washington office sent some researchers to the district to see how our system worked but by the time they got there we had already found a cheaper solution.

We were always strapped for cash and I looked at everything we spent money on. A couple of my efforts upset a few of my staff and caused some issues. We had a couple head of horses, which were seldom used, and were expensive to feed and pasture all winter. It was a tradition in Region 2 to have horses on the districts, but money for project work was more important.

My love for horses was also cooling. Since our horses were pastured all winter, they were a bit on the wild side and posed a danger to our summer employees unfamiliar with horses. Then one day I was riding with a young lady, fresh out of college, and when we were wiping our animals down she stepped behind her horse and was kicked in the stomach and appeared to be badly hurt. I rushed her to a doctor in Leadville, Colorado, but fortunately she wasn't in serious condition. That was the last straw and I transferred the horses to another district and lined up an outfitter to provide stock, as needed, at far less cost and much better trained.

I also cut way back on winter "snow ranger" time on the ski areas. It may have been good public relations, but the money was needed for the summer to oversee construction work that potentially could cause resource damage. For the most part people adjusted, but I had at least one staff member who was upset, and we had a couple of incidents.

I owned a sailboat that I kept in the Dillon marina. One day I got a call from the sheriff and he asked whether my boat had been stolen. I looked out the window from my office and said, "No, it's there." It turns out a couple of my people had thought they were taking my boat and gotten someone else's. They put it on my trailer and drove it up the mountainside on a four-wheel drive road. Fortunately, the owner of the boat didn't press charges. The sheriff knew who did it, but I didn't say a word to them.

Shortly after that, the new Chief of the Forest Service, John McQuire, Regional Forester Bill Lucas, and my boss Don Biddison were to meet District Ranger Paul Wachter and myself at his office in Kemmling, Colorado. I arrived early and looked up to see painted across the front of the office, "DILLON SUCKS." It seems my crew had played Kemmling's crew in softball the night before and some of the same boat thieves were at it again. I rushed into the office and told Paul to look outside. We hatched a plan to get the dignitaries to come in the back door, which worked. The next day I called a little meeting and told the thieves they were good people, but this was their last chance. We didn't have any more problems.

One day, my assistant ranger, Pat Lynch, came in with an unbelievable story. As he was making his rounds he saw a lady with a hand axe beating on an outhouse door. She was screaming, "my boy's in there." The door was locked, and Pat broke the door open only to see this little blond head sitting on the waste in the tank. He reached down and pulled the boy out. His mother ran to the water pump and washed her crying son off. Pat said the last thing he saw was the lady racing out of the campground in her car. That was half the fun of being on a district in the Forest Service—anything can happen.

Straight Creek was running brown from sediment with each passing year, and another attempt was being made by the highway department to stop Interstate Highway 70 from ending up 300 feet down the mountain side. The Colorado Highway Department was fast approaching a more difficult geologic soil problem on Vail Pass only a few miles farther west. They had been discussing several different alternatives but the one they thought might work was expensive. That was to split lane the highway with one lane on the south side of the valley and the other on the north side.

We had a meeting with the chief design engineer, and my boss, Don Biddison, to review the highway department options. When they discussed the split lane option, they thought we would object based on the amount of national forest land that would be impacted. However, we were all for that alternative and argued that another Straight Creek was unacceptable. If done right, with bridges over the streams and a minimum of soil disturbance, it could be an asset to recreation. The bridges could provide access under the interstate for public use and if they put in a rest area at the top of the pass it could provide both summer and winter recreation opportunities. I wasn't sure they would agree to the rest area, but they did, and the department approved that alternative.

I also pushed for a split lane from Copper Mountain Ski Area back to Frisco, Colorado through Ten Mile Canyon. The highway department agreed with me, but as it turned out the archeological review indicated an old Chinese village existed in the path of the south lane. The Chinese laborers, back in the 1800s, were forced to segregate themselves from the other miners and laborers who worked in the valley. They lived in rock huts in this narrow and cold canyon.

The last thing I tried to promote was a bike path running beside the interstate from Frisco to Vail Pass. The local highway engineers were in favor of it but skeptical that the head of the highway department in Denver would go for it. I contacted the regional office and got a lady to come out and film a video for me. This was an attempt to show the value of the bike path. I tried to use the same reporting style that my television friend had used. I must admit it was a bit crude. I talked about the merits of the bike path, then got on a bike and road down the highway. Later I went into to Denver and gave a presentation to the Regional Forester Bill Lucas and the head of the highway department. I showed the video and much to my surprise they approved the idea. I left the district before the design and construction took place but found out later a new employee to the district had taken it upon himself to see that the bike path got built. Years later my old friend Chuck McConnell mailed me a T-shirt they had produced for the dedication of the bike path. The district employee got all the credit and rightly so, but Chuck said in a note, "You should be proud that you were the one who had the idea and got it approved and moving." I appreciated that.

Much had happened in such a short time. By August of 1972 the regional forester gave me an award for my efforts on the Dillon District. The award was for "exceptional managerial competence in achieving desired cooperative relations with Summit County and in organizing and managing the Dillon District, with its complex problems." I had received several awards for my work as a landscape architect, but this was the one I most cherished. At least that's what I thought.

Shortly after receiving this award I was told I would be moving to a newly created job, as the regional planner, in the regional office in Lakewood, Colorado. I had been on the Dillon District just shy of two years and had great hopes for the future with Summit County. I was about to finalize the county zoning regulations with Bob Arceri and hated to suddenly walk away. I pleaded with my boss and the regional forester to let me stay at least until the end of the year. The regional forester already had picked my replacement but agreed to have him work as my assistant until the new year started. His name was Jim Blankenship. It worked out well as I could finish my task with the county and introduce Jim to everyone.

Of all my jobs with the U.S. Forest Service, over thirty-five years, being a district ranger in Summit County, Colorado was the greatest. I made many friends and had some great moments and experiences. As we were packing up to leave they asked that Gretchen and I attend a party at the Copper Mountain Ski Lodge put on by the Summit County Citizens Association. The place was packed with all our friends and elected officials. They presented me with the "Summit Cup," a bronze statue, for efforts at improving relationships with the county and supporting land use planning. The statue sits on my mantel and is my most cherished award.

JAMES L. OGILVIE
Secretary-Manager

Board of Water Commissioners

144 West Colfax Avenue   Denver, Colorado 80202   Phone 222-5511
COMMISSIONERS
WILLIAM G. TEMPLE, President   JOHN A. YELENICK, 1st Vice-President
ANDREW HORAN, JR.,   A. ASBORNO   CHARLES F. BRANNAN

January 10, 1973

Mr. James Hagemeier
U. S. Forest Service
Denver Federal Center
Denver, Colorado 80225

Dear Jim:

Congratulations on being named a recipient of the "Summit Cup"
award made by the Summit County Citizens Association.

In this day and age, where "establishment" government agencies
are suspect by citizen groups generally, you should be particularly
proud of receiving such a tribute by citizens of the county in which
you served so ably for the Forest Service.

In my previous work with the Bureau of Reclamation and now as
Manager of the Denver Water Department, your cooperation has
always been most admirable. We here at the Water Department
are looking forward to continuing working with you in your new
assignment at the Denver office.

The Board of Water Commissioners join with me in congratulating
you on the award and also for being selected for the Denver Post
Gallery of Fame.

Sincerely,

Jim Ogilvie

J. L. Ogilvie, Manager

JLO/br

My greatest award: the Summit Cup

Presented by the Summit County Citizens Association December 30, 1972, in appreciation for outstanding service to Summit County,

CHAPTER 14

ROCKY MOUNTAIN REGION

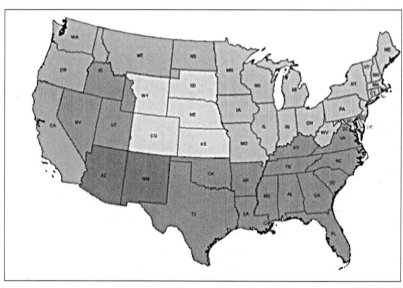

The Rocky Mountain Region is shown in light gray above;
the headquarters are in Lakewood, Colorado

W E HAD A LOVELY HOME in Dillon at the ranger station. It sat on a hill overlooking Dillon Reservoir and the peaks of the Gore–Eagles Nest Wilderness Area in the background. Unfortunately, we were not gaining any equity because it was a government-owned dwelling. We decided to buy a condo with friends of ours, the Schnabels, at Copper Mountain Ski Area. It wasn't going to be completed until early 1973. No sooner had we signed the contract than we moved. We ended up keeping the condo and carrying two mortgages for five years.

My new office in the Rocky Mountain Regional Office was in the Denver Federal Center. Gretchen and I bought a brand-new home on 6th Ave West about one mile from the center.

Our home was nice but had mud for a yard. I designed a landscape plan and worked day and night on the yard. Bob Arceri gave me his Colorado State Nursery license, which let me buy plant materials at wholesale price. That was a huge savings. Retail was three times higher than wholesale on plant materials. I bought a new Ford pickup and proceeded to go to the nursery and fill it with plant materials every weekend. The plants that I didn't use I would give to my neighbors at cost.

A Planner with Nothing to Plan

The yard and house kept me occupied, as I had a tough time figuring out my new job. I was called the regional planner, but I didn't know what I was supposed to plan. I worked for Clayton Peirce, a very nice gentleman. He was the multiple use coordinator for the region. Again, I didn't know what he was supposed to do. My office was right next to Regional Forester Bill Lucas and the Assistant Regional Forester Basil Crane. Bill was a tough boss, but he treated me fairly. Basil didn't say much, but he was well-respected. It became apparent that one of my duties was to be a gopher for Bill. He would ask me to run down and tell a staff director something, which would infuriate the staff director and was awkward for me.

Bill had an interest in forest planning and had fostered several planning efforts on the forests in the region. At least that gave me an excuse to visit these units and see how they were proceeding. They had good people assigned to the task, but in my estimation, they didn't know what they were doing. They didn't have a clear vision of what the final product would look like and were going in circles doing inventories without knowing what their management problems were or what their decisions were going to be. I tried to give them some basic concepts modeled after urban planning concepts I had learned in school. Probably with very little success.

As it turned out, the issue of what decisions are made at each level of planning was one of the bigger problems facing the Forest Service. The later-published National Forest Planning Regulations still didn't clarify this issue, and it wasn't until legal challenges after forest plans were completed that this was defined. From when I first started working in this area as a regional planner, the confusion lasted over twenty years.

What was really unsettling to me was that the forest staff would come into our office to make a presentation to the regional forester, and he would rip them apart. They had done the best they could do and went home discouraged. I think Bill was searching for a solution without knowing what it should look like.

The Forest Service was living through a lawsuit that could only be solved by an act of Congress. It was the Monongalia lawsuit over the use of clear cutting as an option for timber management. Rather than just amend the enabling act of the Forest Service, there was an effort in Congress to have the Forest Service embark on a totally new planning system. This took years to develop and I think Bill Lucas wanted to come up with a solution to offer to Forest Service Chief McQuire. It wasn't until a few years later that I came to this conclusion.

Before long Bill gave me new marching orders. He assigned me to be an informal assistant to a state senator from Colorado. This senator was a driving force in attempting to get land use planning done throughout the state. He went to every county in the state talking with the public about the need to plan and what it could do for them. No easy task. I was his assistant and handled the logistics. Fortunately, I didn't have to give any speeches. We used a Forest Service plane and pilot and toured the state. I accompanied him to all the counties that contained national forest land.

It was an education in several ways. The crowds weren't friendly. Planning was the same as Communism to some people, especially in the small rural communities of western Colorado. It was interesting to watch how the senator handled the crowd and their issues. I enjoyed the experience, especially talking to ranchers and rural folks about development issues and what was happening in their counties.

I got to know the senator well, and we had many discussions about how he was going to proceed and his perceptions on where things were going.

That state assignment took about a year to complete. In the meantime, I was the regional planner with nothing to plan. For the most part I was planning my own agenda. I spent as much time as I could learning what the current thinking was in land use planning. I took a couple of short courses on ecosystem planning at Colorado State University and listened to theories from the different professors. Some things were new but a lot of what I heard was old news. I also got involved in geographic information systems with the University of Colorado. That was exciting, as I could see how this process would be so much easier to use than doing resource overlays by hand.

There was a lot of interest in the ecosystem planning, particularly in the public sector. I teamed up with Bob Arceri, representing Summit County, and put together a conceptual talk on how ecosystems could be used in evaluating a planning area. I used several examples from my timber sale planning efforts and the work that we had done in Summit County. Through all my landscape work I learned how to incorporate photos and drawings into my presentations, so it wasn't just me talking. It seemed to catch on and we were invited to give our presentation to several outside groups.

One of the groups I talked to was the Colorado Game & Fish Department. They asked me to give a two-day workshop on planning for some of their personnel in Steamboat Springs, Colorado, at the ski area. It was now summer and not many tourists were around. We finished up the first day and the guys were headed to the bar and dinner. I was getting ready for the next day's class and told them I would catch up with them.

By the time I was done it was dark. I decided to take a short cut across a meadow to the bar. As I was walking along I stepped on a skunk. Well the skunk sprayed me from the chest down. For whatever reason, the scent overpowered me, and I couldn't smell a thing.

I knew I must smell bad, so I was going to tell the guys I would call it a night and go back to the hotel. As I entered the entrance to the bar there were two tourists looking at a menu and blocking my way. I said, "Excuse me." They turned away and plastered themselves against the wall with a horrified look on their faces. As I entered the bar the bartender yelled, "There's a skunk in here." People started to panic. I walked to the table where a couple of my group were sitting and told them I would not be joining them. They nodded their heads in agreement.

By then the bar was emptying out and I joined them quickly going in the opposite direction. At the hotel, I stripped off my clothes and took several showers. I was now picking up the smell, so I put everything in the trash bin except my belt, shoes and coins. I then put on a clean T-shirt and shorts and went to the desk. Even then the clerk backed up with that look on her face. I asked if they had any tomato juice and she shook her head "no." I asked if they had any Snappy Tom tomato juice and she went to the bar, which was closed, and brought all they had. After a bath in juice and more showers I was back to normal. I got ribbed by the group the next day. Days later the items I saved still smelled like skunk.

When we moved back to Denver, Gretchen got her old job back with the Cherry Creek School District and worked about a year before we had our first child, Heidi. Heidi was a joy and Gretchen quit her job to raise her. We had settled into Denver and still had many old friends in town. Gretchen, being a big sports fan, trotted down to the Denver Broncos office and bought season tickets. We held on to those tickets for thirty-five years through all our moves and would sell the seats to friends.

An Unexpected Change

I was now going on my second summer in the regional office. One day Bill Lucas asked me what I wanted to do in the future. I told him if I was to go anywhere in the Forest Service, I needed to learn more about timber management. At that time timber was still king. Most of Region 2 was not timber country, and what little I had learned wouldn't help me much in trying to move on to another region.

Not long after that Basil Crane, the assistant regional forester, asked me to accompany him and Bill Worth, the head of timber management in the Washington office, on a review of the Black Hills National Forest timber program. The Black Hills was the premier timber forest in the region and had one of the best programs in the country. We spent a week on the forest reviewing their program in the offices and on the ground. We covered every district and I met all the rangers and most of their primary staff. They had to wonder why this landscape architect was along. So did I. Everyone was polite, but there probably was a lot of barroom talk. I thought it was a good week and I learned a lot.

It wasn't long before I got a call from the regional personnel officer to come and see him. I went to his office and he said Bill Lucas had called him and wanted to offer me the resource staff officer position on the Black Hills National Forest. I had to make up my mind by the end of the day. It turns out the present administration had put a freeze on promotions and the job promoted me to a GS-13. If I took the job it would have to be today. I was shocked, again, and immediately called Gretchen. She asked what Custer, South Dakota, was like and I said it's not much. For me it was no problem but for a city girl it would be a problem. I was thrilled, she was apprehensive.

I had no idea the job was even available. The former deputy forest supervisor had been promoted and moved to Region 6 in Oregon and instead of filling his job they had decided to switch to four staff positions. I was to be the new staff in charge of all the resources. The others were engineering, administration, and public affairs/planning. This was going to be another big challenge and another change in course.

We immediately took a house-hunting trip to Custer. It was very depressing. I went to a realtor's office and she asked how much we were willing to spend. I was hoping to get $35,000 out of our house in Denver and wanted to reinvest all of it so I wouldn't have to pay taxes on the profit. The realtor said, "There isn't a house in Custer worth $35,000, honey." She showed us around and she was right. We even looked at a house with dirt floors that was described as a fixer-upper. We finally looked at a house that was livable but ugly and didn't have a garage. In desperation, we made an offer through a realtor and flew back to Denver. While on the plane we looked at each other and said no way. As soon as the plane hit the ground I called the realtor and asked him if they had signed the offer. He said he was on the way for the signature, but they had accepted it. I told him to tear it up. He said you can't do that. I insisted that I could. The contract was voided. Now we had a move and no place to live. Also, we had not sold our house in Denver.

I moved up to Custer in September and got a room in a motel. The tourist season was over, so the owners were willing to give me a long-term rental. It didn't have cooking facilities except for a hot plate. It wasn't fun. In the meantime, my realtor in Denver had not even shown our house. He had been a friend of mine in the Forest Service and had quit to make his millions in real estate. Unfortunately, as I found out, he wasn't very good at it.

As I got acquainted in Custer I met the local attorney, Jerry Baldwin. He called me and asked me to come to dinner. We had a nice evening at his home, which he had remodeled, and toward the end of the night asked if I might be interested in buying his house. "Of course," I said. He had done an excellent job on the remodel, with a sunken living room, gas fireplace a huge garage and three bedrooms. He had even hired the landscape architect from the Forest Service to design his yard. His price also matched my budget. In the end, I sold that house for more money than I ever made on any house I owned.

When I went back to Denver I fired my realtor friend and hired a realtor who had the best sales record in the city of Denver. He sold our house in two weeks.

Our move to Custer, South Dakota must have been a terrible trip for Gretchen. It was a cold, windy trip through Wyoming to a house she had never seen, driving our car with a year-old baby. I think she was questioning my judgment.

CHAPTER 15

THE BLACK HILLS NATIONAL FOREST
RICH IN HISTORY

Oil painting by Leslie Hagemeier, 1976

THE BLACK HILLS National Forest, in my opinion, is one of the premier forests in the National Forest System. I thought so in 1974 when I moved there, and I think so today. It is unique in so many ways. The history of the area surrounds you: the native tribes, General Custer's visit, the gold rush days of Deadwood, Mount Rushmore, and the public support it generated as the only National Forest in South Dakota. It had a longstanding history of excellent management. I was very blessed to have been able to spend time there. It was a meaningful change in my career, a new beginning.

The forest supervisor at the time I arrived was Dave Johns. Dave had moved there from another forest in Colorado not long before I arrived. This seemed strange to me as Dave was towards the end of his career and this move was a major promotion for him. From what I learned of Bill Lucas he always had a reason for what he did. The Black Hills National Forest had the biggest work load and budget in Region 2. Many folks in the region called them Region 2½. Now the forest had a forest supervisor at the end of his career and a new staff officer that was a landscape architect. It must have been demoralizing to the employees.

I spent my first few weeks getting to know my staff and the district people. I didn't have an agenda and just wanted to see where they were coming from and where they might want to go. Generally, I thought my staff was strong, especially in range, fire, and lands. The district rangers were generally good.

During my time working for Dave, I only had one incident that was disturbing. Next to Custer, South Dakota, a developer and sculptor, Korczak Zioikowski, had built a tourist attraction, the Crazy Horse Memorial, with a museum and a rock sculpture of the Sioux warrior. He wanted to build a road on national forest land to further promote his attraction and had not gotten much encouragement from the district ranger or my lands staff. He stepped the pressure up and invited Dave Johns to dinner to try to influence him into allowing the road. Dave asked me to also attend since the lands program was within my responsibility.

The first thing Zioikowski did was take two bottles of liquor and pour them in a bowl. I believe they were called stingers. As I sipped a glass, Dave and Korczak proceeded to drink the entire amount. His wife served our dinner, but he treated her like a maid. She didn't even sit with us. By the end of dinner, my boss and Korczak were feeling the effects of the fancy drinks. I helped Dave out to our car and drove him home. I then helped him up to his front porch and left. I'd seen some heavy drinking in the Forest Service but nothing like this.

It wasn't long after that incident that Dave announced his retirement. The regional forester named me as the acting forest supervisor. Another blow to the forest?

The first thing I did was call all the district rangers together and discussed where we would like to be when the new forest supervisor was named. This was an opportunity for us to set a new course if we were all together. They bought into it and decided they wanted to focus on a more open budget system with more input from the districts. Having gone through a similar effort on the Arapaho National Forest, I was all for it. By the time the new forest supervisor arrived we had accomplished our goal. This meant taking some responsibility away from the supervisor's office staff and giving it to the districts.

While still the acting forest supervisor, Bill Lucas called me and wanted me to come down to Denver and explain how I thought forest planning should be done. He asked the same thing of another National Forest supervisor. I assumed Bill was still on his agenda to influence the Washington office on how the new forest planning process should be handled. I asked Tony Vander Heide, from the planning staff, to put together a concept and make the presentation. I coached Tony on what my vision was, which included dividing the National Forest into management units with each unit having specific goals and management direction—like what we did for the Tahoe Basin Recreation Plan back in 1970. I envisioned it being like a city plan with different land uses and zoning requirements.

It looked like this was going to be another one of Bill's tests, so I knew what to expect. We made our presentation; then the other unit made theirs. Their concept was identical to the existing multiple use plans where most of the forest was in the general management zone and where all resources could be managed as the line officer saw fit. This allowed the manager to make all the decisions without the public knowing what the resource priorities were. Since all resources aren't equal, some took on less importance based on a line officer's judgement. Bill applauded their effort and said our solution took too much decision-making out of the district rangers' hands.

I suspected that was going to be the outcome of our exercise and wasn't really bothered by it. As I saw it, the demands on National Forest lands were growing and people would someday demand to know how every acre was going to be managed. It turns out that day was fast approaching. Congress soon passed the National Forest Management Act of 1976, which influenced the rest of my career.

Spring came, and a new forest supervisor arrived from Oregon. His name was Jim Overbay. He was a very impressive person and I liked him immediately. Jim was very sensitive to public and employee values. It was a pleasure working for Jim, and I learned a lot about managing people. He was also supportive of the budget process the management team had developed and helped to strengthen it. It didn't take Jim long to size up our management team and decide how he wanted it improved.

Jim had heard that Bill Lucas could be difficult to work with and took extra time to get acquainted with Bill and make him feel that we wanted to be supportive of the rest of the region. It worked well. Bill let us run the forest without much interference. Bill also gave me an award as acting forest supervisor, despite my forest plan incident.

Timber or Resource Management Plan?

Not long after Jim Overbay got there, the timber management staff director in the regional office wanted Jim, my timber staff, and me to come to Denver. The staff had earlier sent in a new timber management plan for review. Essentially, they said it was not satisfactory and would have to be done over. They also said that we would have to write an environmental impact statement to comply with the National Environmental Policy Act recently passed by Congress. In private they told Jim that his timber staff was not capable of doing the job. Jim asked if I could do it and I said I'd try. I knew little about timber management, but I did know how to organize a planning effort.

The planning effort centered on a recently developed linear computer program called Timber Ram. Essentially what the program did was take a selected group of timber prescriptions and apply them to the existing inventory of timber stands on the forest. The program then grows the stands over time with the results being how much timber could be harvested over several decades without destroying the forest by overcutting. As I found out, the secret was to clearly define the different goals of management you wanted to achieve on the forest and then translate those goals into timber growth patterns to achieve them. I could organize the effort but had to have the skills to put it all together.

My timber staff was John Windsor. John knew timber and could provide the technical advice to the effort, but I needed other skills as well—in particular, operations research skills. Operations research is a discipline that was brought on by the computer age. In this case, a person who could take an everyday concept such as a timber prescription and convert it into language that would fit into the Timber Ram linear program. There were very few people with those skills in the Forest Service and probably the only people who did have them would have to have a master's degree specializing in that area. I had learned some of these concepts in Colorado State University's short courses but didn't know how to make them work.

Before I got this assignment, I visited a timber sale and talked to a young forester, Paul Ruder, who had just graduated from college with a master's in operations research skills. I reached out and had him reassigned to the forest supervisor's office. I felt we needed wildlife expertise and was able to hire a biologist who also had a working knowledge of silviculture. With the help of several of my staff and district foresters, we started to lay the groundwork for our planning effort.

The Black Hills is a unique ecosystem in that it is primarily one evergreen species, Ponderosa pine. We were fortunate in that for years the area had been studied by research scientists at the Forest Service Research Lab in Rapid City, South Dakota. The scientists there had done studies on how to best thin trees and what benefits could be obtained, such as how much forage for cattle or wildlife would grow based on how much sunlight was available. We could incorporate the models they had already built into our computer program.

In developing our goals, we gathered the specialists together and listed all the benefits that could be derived from managing the trees on the forest. Of course, there are wood products, but we also determined that thinning at a certain level could provide a fire break to more easily control wildfires and those same levels of thinning could provide forage for cattle and wildlife. Total removal of trees could expand meadows and encourage bourse for wildlife. One of the things I insisted on was preserving the large yellow bark pines along our highways for the viewing public. We put all this information together and developed alternatives to incorporate into the computer.

The last part of our job was documenting our findings in the environmental impact statement. I took the lead on that. I wanted to make it more than board feet of timber, but to reflect how the past dictated the future and how other resources could benefit. We were blessed with the photos that were taken by General Custer's visit to the hills in 1876 and the recent book that showed the same locations and the changes that had taken place, some good and some bad. We explained how towns like Deadwood and Whitewood got their names because of the early wildfires and mountain pine beetle attacks. I also found a lady who worked in one of our offices who was an artist and she drew pictures of some of the history and concepts. After completion, we developed a slideshow to show to the interested groups of publics and employees. We went across the state of South Dakota and made our presentation to civic groups, industry and environmental groups.

While the timber management plan wasn't a land use plan per se, the decisions could dictate how the land would be managed in certain situations. The overall goal was to determine the amount of timber that could be cut without overcutting the forest. Of course, under the Multiple Use Act requirements, the timber plan could not degrade the other values. I tried to incorporate both goals. No one argued about the sustainable yield of timber. But they were slower to protect or enhance other forest values—more so the Forest Service employees than the public. But then again, the managers accepted it, as they felt the rapidly changing public attitudes.

There was resentment to my involvement in the process. I was just a reflection of their not knowing what a landscape architect was, a flower planter to them. Seems like I remember Arthur Carhart saying the same thing in his writings. By now I was tough skinned after my early years working to be accepted as a landscape architect, the bitterness I experienced when I became a district ranger, and now being in charge of the timber program on the biggest timber forest in Region 2. I had left my school profession long ago and now I worked for the organization and its mission. I was rewarded for that.

Recently Jim Furnish, a retired Forest Service employee, stopped by my home in Missoula, Montana. Jim had been in the forest supervisor's office while I was on the forest. He gave me a book he published of his memoirs. In the book, *Toward a Natural Forest*, he referenced my involvement in the timber management plan. The following is his opinion.

> About 1975, Jim Hagemeier arrived as the staff officer in charge of the Black Hills timber management program. A landscape architect, Hagemeier was one of the first few non-foresters to crack the ranks of district ranger. Hagemeier had been handpicked by someone but likely not the forest supervisor. Sending a landscape architect to the Black Hills to run the timber program was strongly symbolic—at best provoca-

tive, at worst simply dumb. I heard many foresters grumbling, jaws tightened with resentment, about how wrong it was to send us a "know nothing."

From day one, Hagemeier let it be known that he pursued a new mission. He made it be clear that he had his eye on a beautiful stretch of US Highway 385 just south of Pactola Reservoir that meandered through a gorgeous creek bottom with tall grass and pretty "yellow bellies," big mature pines whose bark had aged to a sublime yellow-orange that was beautiful from afar. Get real close to a big pine and you can smell the aroma—a spicy vanilla-esque scent. It has thick, fire-resistant bark that easily flakes off in your hand, each piece unique as a snowflake. People like Ponderosa pine forests—they are simply beautiful at an elemental level.

Until Hagemeier arrived, these big old Black Hills pines had a well-known destination: a nearby sawmill. Ponderosa pine lumber has strength, easy workability, rich grain, occasional knots to give it character and thus, a very high value. There exists an implicit agreement—between foresters and trees (even trees that have no say)—when a tree gets to a certain size, well . . . it's had a good long life, plenty of kids, only gonna be downhill from here, so "adios!" But Hagemeier insisted that these beauties stay put.

I heard Hagemeier argue his case passionately and persistently. I saw the reaction both to his face and behind his back and it reflected bitterness, resentment and more than a little fear. He and others like him were beginning to question the agency's fundamental values. These internal voices were reflective of a growing storm outside the Forest Service.

Years later I had a good friend, John Twiss, who had been the forest supervisor on the Black Hills for ten years. I asked him about the timber program and some of the things I tried to build into it. I mentioned the fire prescription, the meadow clearing for wildlife purposes, and leaving the big yellow bark Ponderosa pines along the highway. He said although they still advocate clearing meadows of trees, leaving the big yellow bark trees along the major highways was a prescription they all embraced. One ranger had really gone out of his way to make it happen. Some things take time. In Montana, several National Forests are now protecting and enhancing old growth "yellow belly" Ponderosa Pine in areas viewed by the public.

Jim Furnish captured my greatest concerns. I had now worked for the Forest Service for twenty years. I knew the culture and its mission of multiple use. I also knew that timber management didn't need any help. It ruled. It was the other multiple uses and forest values that needed help. My experience in Colorado entrenched this vision. The public there were upset about our management and made their values known. I thought I was doing my part to minimize impacts caused by developments but was taken back by Aldo Leopold's daughter's bitter attack during my presentation on scenic management years earlier.

During development of the Black Hills timber management plan, I wasn't consumed by protecting big Ponderosa pine—I wanted to promote the idea that management of the forest landscape could enhance many values, not just produce timber products. That's the message I hoped to sell to the public and my bosses. My boss Jim Overbay and the regional forester agreed with both the concept and the results.

Whatever Forest Service organization I was then assigned to, I met outstanding people. I was very fortunate to meet many. On the Black Hills, there were several worth mentioning. One was a young man named Larry Gadt. Larry was at that time working on an interagency exchange program at an African-American university in Alabama. On his own he had traveled to the Black Hills to see if there might be some future job opportunities. We spent some time talking and I was impressed. We had a district ranger's job that would soon be vacant, and Jim Overbay agreed we should try to fill the job with Larry. Which we did. Larry did an outstanding job as the Custer District ranger. Our paths crossed several times, since he ended up as a director in the Washington office.

Years before I had met a young forester on the district next to mine when I was a ranger, Fred Trevey. Fred had become a district ranger in Colorado but when I was on the Hills he said he was having problems with his forest supervisor. We had a district ranger whose background was in range management and wanted to get back to Colorado. I talked to Overbay about Fred and highly recommended him. Jim worked out a trade and Fred became our new district ranger at Spearfish, South Dakota. Fred went on to become a forest supervisor in Region 1 and then 3.

One day, Jim Overbay came to my office and asked if I would go to a landscape architecture conference in Aspen, Colorado. He had met a young lady by the name of Wendy Herrett. She was a landscape architect on a forest in Region 6. He thought with some experience she could be the first woman district ranger in the Forest Service. I arranged to give a talk at the conference and met Wendy. I agreed with Jim that she had a lot of potential. We ended up hiring her and put her under a good mentor on the Rapid City District. Wendy when on to become the first woman district ranger, then a forest supervisor, and the director of recreation in Region 6.

In the fall of 1976, Bill Lucas retired and a new regional forester, Craig Rupp, took over the region. He came from the Washington office, where he had been director of planning, and had some definite ideas on how planning should be done. He came to the Black Hills on a visit and I gave him a presentation on our timber management planning process. He had several criticisms, and I didn't know where he was coming from. I had high hopes of getting a deputy forest supervisor job sometime in the future. With Lucas I had a chance, but I wasn't sure with Mr. Rupp.

Area Guides

Before long, Jim Overbay said Craig wanted me to head up the planning for an interregional initiative he was spearheading. The product was going to be called "Area Guides" for Colorado, Wyoming, and portions of the Great Plains, comprising North and South Dakota, and Nebraska. There were to be three teams, one for each area, they would be doing the public outreach and putting together the final product. I would have a team developing the planning concepts and analysis for all the areas.

I wasn't enthusiastic. It would require leaving my family every Monday morning and spending the week in Denver, returning Friday evening. It was supposed to last six months. At the time our daughter Heidi was three years old and our son Andrew, only seven months old. It would be a burden on Gretchen, but I had no choice.

Joining me from the Black Hills was Fred Trevey, who would be on one of the teams. I also drafted a new operations research analyst from our unit to work on any computer programming we had to do. The other team members were also a couple of friends of mine, Pat Lynch, my former assistant at Dillon, Colorado, who was now the district ranger at Encampment, Wyoming, and Larry Larson, who was the present district ranger at

Dillon, Colorado. A good group of capable guys that made our experience worthwhile.

I had to keep asking myself, how do I get into these situations? I had no idea what the analysis was supposed to look like or what the final product would look like. At least with the timber management plan I knew what the target was. We had an out-of-region guy who was supposed to be experienced and was our boss, but we soon found out he was all smoke. I tried my best to get some direction, but it didn't come. I eventually came up with a process and brainstormed it with the whole group. They were supportive, but the ideas were conceptual and needed detail.

I recommended we break the states into very broad ecosystems. Up until now, all the efforts on ecosystem planning had been at a local area. Now we were talking about millions of acres in a unit. Within each area we would then have teams of resource specialists who would inventory the existing situation and make assessments as to opportunities or barriers to increasing goods and services from National Forest Lands. We would then put all this information into a computer program that would essentially add up the costs and benefits of different budget levels or different requirements. Once we had the alternatives structured, we could estimate the effects on resources such as roadless lands, or say, grizzly bears.

In the meantime, our boss had hired a consultant to do the social evaluation. They were an outfit out of Denver called the Foundation for Urban Neighborhood Development, (FUND). The owner was Jim Kent. He talked about how they would map neighborhoods by their social structure. I was fascinated, as it reminded me of the rural sociology courses I had in college about settlement patterns and like cultures grouping together.

Once you identified the neighborhood you would identify the power brokers and gathering places. Using this information, you could identify the issues and how change would affect the neighborhood. Jim Kent's problem is that he couldn't extend his process into the scope of several states. To me it seemed to be like ecosystems, if it worked. If we could identify ecosystems at a large scale why can't we identify social systems at the same scale? He sent his staff out across the Great Plains and said it works. We had folks say exactly where the social system changed down to a river or highway. They then sent crews throughout the states in our planning area and delineated the social units. The idea was to use these areas as a way of obtaining public input, to modify alternatives based on cultural differences, and to pass on possible decisions.

I learned as much from this exercise as anyone. To this day, I believe the Forest Service planning system lacks this important aspect of planning. People's values and perceptions are based on the social system in which they exist. If you try to impose values across the board, you will not be successful. What you end up doing is imposing other people's values on other cultures, which in the long run builds resentments. I believe one reason the Forest Service had been successful in the past is because they put a lot of the decision-making at the local level.

I finally was released to go back to the Black Hills. In the meantime, my boss, Jim Overbay, had been promoted to the Washington office and a new forest supervisor was taking over. I was worn out from my last assignment and hardly returned to my desk when I was told I would be the new deputy forest supervisor on the Ottawa National Forest in the upper peninsula of Michigan. I guess that was my reward, but Regional Forester Craig Rupp did write Gretchen a nice letter thanking her for the sacrifice she had to make. He also said our effort would set a standard for the rest of the Forest Service. This didn't happen, as the new forest planning regulations set a different course for what they called a regional guide.

Ponderosa pine at Council Grove, Montana
Council Grove is a stand of old growth ponderosa pine that have been pro-
tected in Montana as a State Park. Here, Isaac Stevens negotiated the Hell-
gate Treaty between the U.S. government and the Salish, Kootenai, and
Pend d'Oreille Tribes to create the Flathead Reservation in 1855.

CHAPTER 16

THE UPPER PENINSULA OF MICHIGAN

AND

THE OTTAWA NATIONAL FOREST

Oil painting by Leslie Hagemeier

A typical winter day in the Upper Peninsula

IN AUGUST of 1977 Gretchen and I went on a house hunting trip to our new town of Ironwood, Michigan. Ironwood is the headquarters of the Ottawa National Forest in the upper peninsula of Michigan. It's 100 miles from Duluth, Minnesota and over 300 miles from lower Michigan state. The people who lived in the upper peninsula were called Uppers, and very proud that they were the other Michigan. We flew to Duluth over the bright blue skies of the West and drove a rented car to Ironwood. The sky got grayer, and as we approached the town it started to drizzle. We checked into the Holiday Inn and decided to look around before dinner.

Ironwood is an old mining town. The mines were shut down and so was the town. The town was divided in sections based on the location of the mines. As we drove around it was depressing. It was like going to Wales after the mines closed. Boarded up churches, schools and rundown houses. Now you must remember we came from Custer, South Dakota, where there wasn't a house in town worth $35,000. There wasn't a house in Ironwood worth $25,000, and even less after you bought it. Poor Gretchen was crying, and I was sick.

We had a realtor who showed us nothing. I went to the local bank to see what the market might be in the future. There were two ski areas close by and maybe they had a potential for housing. I met with the vice president of the bank, Ed Hunt, who was a young progressive guy. He said he had a house he could rent to us until we found something that met our needs. I jumped at the offer. We at least had a home until we could decide what to do. In late September of 1977 we moved to Ironwood and settled into this 5,000-square-foot foreclosed house. Way more than we needed but a roof over our head. We were about five miles out in the country.

I settled into my job. My office was on US 2 east of town. A new building with a great view of an aspen forest. My boss, the forest supervisor, was Marvin Lawrenson. He had spent his whole career in Region 9, the Eastern Region of the Forest Service. Region 9 extended from Minnesota to Maine and south to West Virginia and Missouri, big and diverse. Marv had been the forest supervisor on the Chippewa National Forest in Minnesota before moving to the Ottawa. It didn't take me long to figure out that the management was years behind my experience in Region 2. Not to put the people down but the times had not caught up with them. They were totally timber orientated, at least on the Ottawa. Other resources were secondary, especially recreation and wildlife. Some of the staff directors were competent—timber, lands and engineering—but it was apparent the rest were placed there because they had either failed or were no longer effective. I could see this would be a challenge I had never faced before.

Back to my house hunting. I had decided if we were going to invest our money in a house it had to be something we could sell. Our track record was that we had moved every two-plus years. Our house had to be new and in an attractive location to be able to sell it.

I proceeded to use the social skills that FUND had taught me in the Area Guide effort. After work I would go to the local taverns, the gathering places that are scattered throughout the countryside, and have a beer with the local Finnish farmers. After a few visits they accepted me enough to talk. My question was, do you know anyone that might be willing to sell me some land for a house? They said see Wano Selin. Wano was up in years and had a large farm.

He was not dumb. When I asked about a piece of land Wano

took me to a dried-up swamp. "Wano, this is a dried-up swamp, right?" "No, it's good farm land." After some conversation, I asked, "What are you going to do with all this land?" He said his dream was to develop a subdivision on the best of it and have it named after him. I said, "I can do that for you. I can design it and get it platted, and I can put a sign up with your name on it." He agreed, and we proceeded to buy the property.

Gretchen was excited to see our new property out in the country. It was a beautiful setting with tall pines on the edge of a long meadow with an outstanding view of the adjacent forest. We drove around and looked at other country homes and Gretchen kept asking questions like, "Why are the garages so far from the house and on the road?" Or, "Why does that house have the lower portion of the roof covered with metal?" Or the worst question, "Why does that house have a door on the second floor with no porch or stairs?" They must get a ton of snow here. I was right, more snow than anyplace I ever lived. It would start snowing the first of November and wouldn't stop. It got to the point my snowblower could no longer blow the snow out of the road bed. It was an adventure.

One night coming home from work in a blizzard I drove into a snowbank that covered my truck. I was in trouble, couldn't move, and knew I didn't dare try to walk. Just then I saw the lights of a snowplow approach. The driver pulled me out and plowed a lane to my home.

My next challenge was getting a house built. I couldn't find a building contractor in the county. Gretchen heard of a fellow who sold and put together pre-cut homes. His name was Jim Novak. I contacted Jim and looked at his products. Jim had recently married his wife Pat, and they had moved to Indianhead Ski Area to build condos. Business was slow, so he got into the pre-cut home business. I think I was his first customer. The homes were pre-cut in Wisconsin then shipped in sections to the construction site. When done, they looked like a stick-built home. We went with it.

It was wild. Jim is a character, and I enjoyed taking my lunch hour and joining the crew. With my construction background I inspected every aspect, which I think made Jim nervous. One day I came out to see how they were doing putting the second floor on. They had it on and the crane had left. Something was not right, so I looked at the plans and told Jim, "It's on backwards. The overhang should be on the other end." Jim laughed it off and said he could make it work. My comment was no you can't, move it back. So, he had to jack the second floor up, put rollers under the joists and rent a caterpillar to pull the second floor to its correct position. We finally got it done and moved into it in mid-February 1978. Jim and Pat ended up being some of the best friends we have ever had, and still have.

All these months, I had been watching the forest supervisor and how he operated. The forest supervisor's focus was on timber. I thought my contribution to the forest's management could best be served with my background in recreation and wildlife management. I spent time visiting the districts and getting to know the district rangers and their staffs. One good thing about my visits is the Forest Service employees didn't know I was a landscape architect by profession. I had now been in three jobs over the last seven years as a forester. While being a landscape architect may have been an issue in Region 2, it was no longer. I remained in the forestry series for the rest of my career.

It was obvious that the forest had a terrific opportunity for fish and wildlife management. The forest was covered with lakes and the Michigan Department of Natural Resources didn't have the funds to do much in the way of management. Traditionally the Forest Service did not do fish habitat management but there was no law against it.

The forest also had an overstory of primarily hardwood, maples and assorted species. A lot of the early stage species, such as aspen, were disappearing and with them a decline in associated wildlife species. The forest emphasis was on the hardwoods because of their timber value.

While on the Black Hills we were promoting the re-establishment of aspen and had invited Doctor Gordon Gullion, a research scientist from the University of Minnesota, to meet with our field people. He was a wildlife biologist by training but was advocating aspen management as a key to increasing certain wildlife values. He put on seminars for our employees and they started to incorporate his ideas into their timber programs.

I approached Marv about trying to put on the same sessions for our people. It turns out he had issues with this scientist when he was the forest supervisor on the Chippewa National Forest. He was not for it.

That spring Regional Forester Steve Yurick called Marv to tell him he wanted to spend a week on the forest to visit all the districts and see how things were going. Marv was beside himself and extremely nervous. Steve had a reputation of being a tough regional forester, though he was widely admired for being fair. He was reputedly an impressive man who looked like Abraham Lincoln both in facial appearance and stature. I had never met the man but knew he had been the regional forester in Region 1, Montana, before moving to the Region 9 headquarters in Milwaukee, Wisconsin.

Steve arrived, and we started the rounds of all the districts. I drove, with Steve in the front seat and Marv in the back. Steve asked me about my background, and I said I had started in the Forest Service in fire and had been a smokejumper. It turns out his career had been in fire and having been in Montana he managed the smokejumper program. He had been raised in a coal mining town outside of Steamboat Springs, Colorado, and grew up fishing the Flat Top Primitive Area. That's where I started, so we talked about all the lakes we had fished. All this time Marv couldn't get a word in edgewise, and Steve, who was focused on meeting people and talking about the district employees' ideas to improve management, didn't seem a bit interested in Marv's program of work. I liked Steve and we got along.

Opportunity Knocks

Not long after that, Marv was transferred to Tennessee in Region 8. I was named acting forest supervisor, and the new forest supervisor would not arrive for six months.

I gathered all the district rangers together and said this is our opportunity to set a new course of management, if we work together. To a person they wanted to strengthen our wildlife program. We had one wildlife biologist who was ready to retire and had not been effective in working with the districts.

I wanted a strong program and experienced leadership. I contacted the Michigan Department of Resources and Conservation and suggested an interagency personnel appointment of one of their top biologists for a two-year assignment. They agreed and my recreation staff officer, Bob Burton, and I went to Lansing, Michigan, to interview their candidates. We spent an entire day interviewing and had a couple of potential candidates. It was about quitting time and this fellow stuck his head in the door and said he had talked to some of the others and liked what we were saying. He asked if he could interview. His name was Dan Tucker and he fit my idea of a good manager. He had experience, was soft spoken and advocated changing our timber program to better incorporate wildlife values. He had managed a state forest and had hands-on experience on how to do just that. Lastly, he suggested we approach the Department of Natural Resources about incorporating their fish management program into our habitat management program, which we did. He was our man.

I called Dr. Gullion and asked if he would put on a seminar for our field people on aspen management. He agreed. It was a big success. Our potential to manage aspen was huge and if done right could increase a number of wildlife species. One, ruffed grouse, could be an opportunity to encourage out-of-state hunters to visit our forest, which would provide economic benefits to our communities.

With the advent of chip board products made from aspen chips the timber industry could be the catalyst to do the work, but we needed wildlife biologists at the district level to help lay out the cutting patterns. The timber sale receipts could cover the cost, but we needed to raise our personnel ceilings to be able to hire biologists. I went to the regional office, with Dan Tucker's help, and outlined our plan and opportunity. The regional forester liked it and we started hiring both wildlife and fisheries biologists.

When my new boss, Bob Tippiconi, arrived, our program was humming. Fortunately, Bob was supportive. Bob was a full-blooded Comanche Indian and had been raised on a reservation in New Mexico. He was soft spoken, a people person and had a strong resource background having been raised on a ranch.

He strongly believed in the importance of public input in our decisions. After visiting all our districts, he came back feeling we needed to strengthen public involvement. I recommended we contract with Jim Kent from FUND to put on a series of training sessions on identifying our neighbors and their needs. He agreed. At first the district rangers thought it was a waste of time but after one session they were on board. After explaining how the process worked, Jim Kent sent the district rangers out to their communities to identify the gathering places, or the places where people informally gather to share information. Since we were talking about very small rural communities, these could be the local church, bar, or filling station. After completing that assignment, they all reported back. The next session was to identify the key community leaders. From these sessions the rangers became more involved in their communities and found ways to support their needs. The program was a remarkable success.

The district rangers had stories to share. One said it was the first time he had gone to church when people stood up and shook his hand. Another told of posting a notice at the gathering places on his district about a project to remove rough fish. Normally, these fish would be destroyed, but the notice offered people the opportunity to take them home. Over fifty cars showed up with people carrying buckets. I had given this district ranger a less than satisfactory rating months earlier. He embraced the program and by July 4th was the person of honor in the local parade. It turned his career around.

I found I was enjoying working on a forest I was first depressed about. I think Gretchen was also feeling better about Ironwood. We had made friends and supported our local church that needed new faces. Our kids were doing well. Heidi had just started school and Andrew was three. Wano would come over and give the kids rides on his tractor. The only thing we needed to watch out for were the bears, which were always wandering through our place.

Dan Tucker had shown me how to hunt for woodcock, a very unusual bird. I did a lot of fishing with Jim Novak. The fishing in the upper peninsula was tremendous with variety from Lake Superior to small trout streams. It was an outdoorsmen's paradise, but I was getting nervous about not getting a forest supervisor job, which was my ultimate career goal. One day my old boss Jim Overbay called me to say that my name kept coming up for forest supervisor jobs at the Washington office, but someone was getting it removed. I never found out who might have removed my name, but Jim thought it was Craig Rupp, my old regional forester from Region 2. I later thought it was Steve Yurick. He had other things in mind.

National Forest Planning

In despair, I applied for a recreation job in the Washington office thinking it would strengthen my chances of getting a forest supervisor job. I got a letter back saying I did not qualify because I was not a forester, but a landscape architect. So, apparently experience didn't count. Besides, I knew very few foresters that had an education in recreation management. Fortunately, that system has been changed.

It was now the winter of 1980. The Washington office was putting on training sessions on how to meet the National Forest Management Act planning requirements. They were holding two-week sessions throughout the country. Every forest with a planning team was required to attend. Our region picked three line officers to attend and critique the session. I was picked as the lead and had two district rangers on my team. We spent two weeks in Duluth, Minnesota, in the winter. How lucky is that?

We listened to high-powered professors talk about the process and requirements. It was like the short course I had taken at Colorado State University. In fact, the contract for the session was with that university. There was little or no discussion of managing the process and ensuring the effort was cost effective. It also put most of the planning burden on what they called the "planning team," a group of specialists that would be sort of like Noah's Ark, except one of each. Most of these folks had never planned anything in their career. The planning concept was heavily relying on a linear computer program called FORPLAN, short for forest planning. From what I knew about the program, it was an expansion of Timber RAM that I had used on the Black Hills timber management plan and the program we used for the area guide exercise. If not managed, it was garbage in and garbage out. Having been through these wars I had concluded that most management problems were not linear, in either scope or solution. I was also concerned that the district rangers be involved in the process and there needed to be strong leadership by the forest and regional management teams. Without their involvement, the solutions they offered might not be feasible. I'm not sure the district rangers on my team understood the issues I raised, but they agreed they needed to be involved. At the end of the session, I essentially laid out our concerns in the critique to the group. Regional Forester Steve Yurich and Deputy Chief Nelson of the Forest Service flew up from Milwaukee for the critique. That didn't bother me, as I felt strongly about what I said.

A month or two went by, and I got a call from the regional office offering a promotion to a GS-14 in their Milwaukee office as the new regional planner in charge of completing forest plans in Region 9.

I turned down their offer. I had been through enough of these planning efforts where you had to start from the beginning. Besides, my goal was to be a forest supervisor and I had sacrificed my family to achieve it.

I then got a letter to move or quit. I was now forty-two years old and I couldn't throw my career away, but I didn't respond to the letter. After a week or so I got a call from Steve Yurich asking me to fly down to Milwaukee and have lunch with him. I thought long and hard about what I was going to say.

As I saw it, the Forest Service, as a decentralized organization, allowed the local units flexibility in how they do their job. While some of that has merit, it had become apparent that too much flexibility can lead to problems. I once heard a Native American Chief say, "Working with the Forest Service is like working with a loose federation of warring tribes." I now felt I was walking into a no-win situation.

We met in a small café on Wisconsin Avenue in downtown Milwaukee. Steve proceeded to tell me how much he needed someone with my experience and how he knew I wanted to be a forest supervisor. He said, "I can make anybody a forest supervisor but there are only a handful of people that can do this job and they are not in this region." I said I would take the job, but I had three conditions. Steve almost exploded out of his chair. "I don't take conditions," he said. "Please hear me out," I said.

My conditions were simple, but controversial. We needed to go out of our way to hire people with the computer skills to run the FORPLAN program on every forest to be successful. Also, I felt we needed to develop guidelines on how to proceed and every forest should be required to follow those guidelines. Lastly, as each forest completed segments of these guidelines, the product would be reviewed in the regional office with a team comprising the regional staff directors. Their job would not be to second-guess the forest supervisor's decisions but to ensure the forest had followed the process correctly. Thankfully, Steve agreed with all my conditions.

CHAPTER 17

THE EASTERN REGION
LANDS NOBODY WANTED

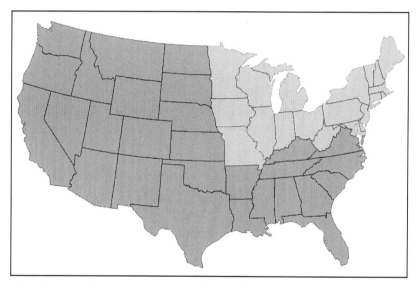

The Eastern Region is shown in light gray on the map above. Parts of these states were lands nobody wanted—forested land with marginal agricultural value. Homesteaders were encouraged to start their lives in these areas but couldn't. They walked away leaving counties with unpaid taxes and a high cost of management. The federal government stepped in and purchased them to create National Forests. They now supply forest products and tremendous recreational opportunities for the public.

I T LOOKED LIKE it was going to take some time to sell our house in Ironwood. There weren't many buyers, if any. I sold my pickup and bought a Volkswagen Rabbit diesel to drive back and forth to Milwaukee, Wisconsin, 300 miles away. My father lived in Racine, so I stayed with him. That was nice, as we had been separated for years. I had found a house in Brookfield, Wisconsin, that I thought was a good buy. Gretchen made it down to house hunt but didn't like the house I found. We decided to wait until we sold our house before we looked for another one.

We were very lucky to have the fellow who replaced me as deputy forest supervisor buy our house. He had two good choices, but our location sold him. We were then able to look for a house in Milwaukee again. Of all the choices, the one I had originally picked out was the one we put a bid on. It had been on the market for a year but was well built and in a nice neighborhood, with the kids' school only blocks away. There was one problem with it—the house had a swimming pool.

Again, we got lucky as the neighbors were great. There were a ton of kids for ours to play with, and the commute to work was easy. I was able to car pool with four men from the office, including Steve Yurick. That gave me a good chance to bounce ideas off him, whereas I might have had a tougher time reaching him in the office.

The office was right on Wisconsin Avenue and not far from Lake Michigan. Neither Gretchen nor I were excited about moving to Milwaukee. We had hoped to be going back out West. Also, I was not a big city boy, and in Milwaukee everyone wore a sports coat or a suit to work. My other problem was there was no hunting within a couple of hundred miles. However, we grew to love Milwaukee with all its activities, schools, and super living conditions.

A Uniform Process

Shortly after I moved to the regional office, I met with the staff directors to organize the regional review process. They were very supportive and wanted to be involved. I then asked all the forest planners to come in, so I could explain the review process and the conditions I agreed to with the regional forester. This included the Superior National Forest, which was supposed to be the lead forest with the idea that it would show the others how to proceed. Staff there had been working on their plan for a year but not effectively. They asked if they were going to be included in our review and I said yes you are. They were not happy, but I said if you have done your job it should be no problem. It seems there were other forests not happy with the process I recommended.

At his first opportunity, one of the forest supervisors came to see the Regional Forester Steve Yurick. He told him he had the skilled people and with his leadership could do the job without the regional office's involvement. Steve told me later that he said, "That's great because Hagemeier really wants to be a forest supervisor so if you're that good we'll trade places." We never heard another peep.

My boss was Jim Freeman. Jim was a very nice man but a bit over his head with all the changes that were taking place. Besides me he had another new GS-14, Jack Cravens, who was supposed to do a regional plan and a new program analyst by the name of Bob Jacobs. Bob was a very bright guy who had just arrived with an advanced degree from Michigan State University.

One of the first things Jim Freeman did was to take me to a planning directors' meeting in Denver. I knew a couple of directors from my area guide effort. I kept my mouth shut as they were engrossed in the technical end of the computer model FORPLAN. I never thought it was the end-all of planning, but primarily a tool to schedule timber volume.

My planning philosophies were totally different. They were based on my education in landscape architecture and city planning mixed with the realities of going through so many different planning efforts in the Forest Service and at the county level in Summit County, Colorado. The last thing I advocated were the tools. The first thing I focused on were the problems facing the land manager. The problems dictated the analysis, and many of the issues in long-range planning were not suited to be addressed by a computer, especially a linear program.

There were a lot of similarities between the requirements in the National Forest Planning Regulations and my background, but those regulations had been written with timber management scheduling in mind and automatically focused on structuring the FORPLAN model. My new challenge was developing planning guidelines based on my background in the field. I broke the process into phases, with the first phase being to identify the management problems. By problems I meant the interactions between similar management issues, public concerns, and opportunities. The listed items were discussed in the regulations but not in the context of their relationship.

The management problems dictated what needed to be measured, the scope of the problem in time and space and what type of external involvement was needed. The last thing the planners would do is determine the type of analysis and tools that they would use. This product would be reviewed in the regional office with all the staff directors. Upon their approval, the forest planning team would move to the second phase.

In this phase, the forests structured their analysis and developed a series of alternatives that would attempt to resolve the management problems and determine where they were applied. The forest planning team then combined solutions into a range of feasible forest-wide alternatives. Again, this was reviewed by the regional staff directors.

The last phase was to do the environmental impact statement and select a preferred alternative, with a final review. All three phases emphasized that the interdisciplinary team involved the district rangers and their staffs. The district rangers were the people that would have to live with the results, and the results had to be feasible.

At first there were objections to all the reviews and even having the regional directors involved. As the process unfolded it brought everyone together and helped them understand the process and the results. At no time did the directors dictate the decisions. Any objections were over logic, and technical input was based on the directors' and their staff's expertise.

As the process unfolded it became apparent that having every forest do their own thing posed a communication problem. The most glaring issue was the numbering system for management areas. It seemed every forest invented their own system, making it difficult to understand the results. I had found this to be true when I was the regional planner in Region 2. As I visited different forests, I was constantly asking what they meant by this or that. I thought we needed a common language for naming management areas for the entire region. This would not only provide a means of communicating intent but later we could have a composite of different kind of management for the entire region. This could be a valuable tool for communications, programming, and budgeting.

I approached Regional Guide Coordinator Jack Cravens with the idea of including a management area structure in the regional guide. He agreed, as he was struggling with just what went into the guide besides clear-cutting standards, as required by regulations. The regional staff directors took the lead and working with forest supervisor input developed a range of management options that the forests could use in structuring their management area prescriptions. As it turned out, not everyone was happy with this arrangement.

The regional forester got a call from the Society for the Protection of New Hampshire Forests, a longstanding and well-respected organization associated with the White Mountain National Forest. They wanted Jack Cravens to come to a meeting with them, the Appalachian Mountain Club, and forest personnel to explain our regional planning and how the management options were going to affect the forest's planning efforts. Jack couldn't go so I took his place.

It had been a while since I had a chance to talk to the public. We had an open and friendly meeting, and the group was comfortable with our process and goals. The spokesman for the groups, Charles W. Burnham, wrote the regional forester complementing him on our approach and said, "A good number of people in the room that day felt a lot more comfortable about the planning process and the regional office role relative to our concerns about the White Mountain National Forest."

We developed a series of management options that framed the diverse types of management one could find on any of our national forests. Region 9 had fifteen national forests with a tremendous variety of ecosystems and cultures from Maine to Missouri. Most of the management area options were described by the various ecological types and the different ways they could be managed. I also argued for an option that recognized what I called "special places." At that time, Region 9 didn't have Wilderness areas except for the Boundary Waters Canoe Area on the Superior National Forest, but they had many unique areas that were major attractions to the public. I knew of a couple that I used as a reference in my arguments. One was the Current River in Missouri where I worked when I got out of high school. The other was the Sylvania tract on the Ottawa National Forest. They were both outstanding areas that needed to be protected. We finally came to agreement on that option.

One of my conditions, hiring people with operations research analyst (ORA) skills, was a challenge. A couple of the units were very aggressive and hired some outstanding people. Others had a tough time. My staff combed field personnel and universities for possible candidates. Usually people with these computer skills had a master's degree and were sought after. Sometimes they would just pop up.

One day, I was leaving the office for lunch when a young man walked up to me on Wisconsin Avenue in downtown Milwaukee and asked if I worked for the Forest Service. When I said I did, he said he had just been talking to personnel in our office about a job. He had recently graduated with a master's degree in wildlife biology, and they told him there were no vacancies for biologists. As we waited for the light to change, I asked him what he specialized in. He said operations research. I took him to lunch and after an hour was very impressed. I took him back to the office, called the Superior National Forest planner, who was still struggling on his plan, and said I have a candidate for you. Within a day, he was hired and turned out to be a tremendous help to that unit.

Not all the analysts worked out, and our regional operations research analyst (ORA), Dan Jones, would visit the units and coach them though the process. But we needed more help. We found an ORA with a doctorate from Colorado State University, Tom Mitchel. We hired him as a temporary employee until we could find a job where his wife was living. We sent him to the Wayne Hoosier National Forest in Indiana to help their team. He helped turn that unit around and did me a favor.

We had all the forest planners and their ORAs in for a meeting in Milwaukee to review and share information on the progress. While I was at the front of the group we had a new employee, who was in the public affairs shop, get up and say I wasn't qualified to be the regional planner. It seems he had just graduated with a master's in planning and this was his first job with the Forest Service. I was speechless. Before I could say a word, Tom Mitchel leaped to his feet and said, "I've got a doctorate in planning and Jim is more qualified than you or anyone else in this room."

Actually, my job was to see the plans got completed, not do them. I admit, being at the front of the pack sometimes was tough. Especially when you're building the plane while you're flying it. It seemed like every job I had was like that. But I learned early on you needed grit and good people to help you. My crew in Region 9 were the best and brightest.

A New Challenge

In 1982, our forest plans were moving along when my boss Jim Freeman announced his retirement. The big question was who was going to replace him. The job was advertised and the closing date for applying was approaching. One day Regional Forester Steve Yurich called me to his office. He wondered why I had not applied for the job. I again said my goal was still to be a forest supervisor. He said he wanted me to apply and promised he would only choose me if there weren't any other good candidates. It wasn't long before I was selected as the new GS-15 Director of Planning, Programming, and Budgeting. Thankfully I had a skilled staff.

An interesting side note to what happened. Recently I was talking to Dale Bosworth, who spent eight years as chief of the Forest Service. It seems Steve Yurich had asked him to apply for the same job. At the time Dale also wanted to be a forest supervisor, but said he applied when Steve told him he was going to select me but needed a good backup. Had Dale gotten the job I might have achieved my career goal as a forest supervisor after all.

As the plans progressed I had the opportunity to visit several of our forests and see how things were going. I tried to time my visits to occur when they had a district ranger meeting mainly to see how the rangers felt about the process and progress. There were a couple of meetings I can still remember, and where I think I may have helped.

On the Green Mountain National Forest in Vermont, one of the significant public issues was clear cutting. The forest is primarily covered with hardwoods. Clear cutting was the forest's primary harvest method. They would get excellent reproduction and it benefited wildlife, but the public hated it. One of the rangers said he had positive response from the public by leaving several older trees like a shelter wood system of management. It reminded me of the big tree prescription I wrote into the Black Hills timber management plan. I spoke up and supported his approach and said with appropriate slash disposal, people would accept it. Whether that conversation made a difference I don't know, but the forest proposed that approach in their final plan and got tremendous public support.

The Superior National Forest had a different problem. They were losing their moose to a disease caused by a parasite that was carried by deer. The biologists told them that the only way to solve the problem was to create very large clearings where the moose could separate themselves from the deer, which could limit the spread of the parasite. Since clear cutting was a regionwide issue with the public, they were concerned about how they would address the moose problem. The regional guide was coming out with directions that would limit clear-cut openings to around fifteen acres and a maximum, in rare cases, of up to forty acres. They needed to go to 200 acres. I strongly supported the 200-acre cuts and said the guide allows for exceptions if justified and I would back them.

I thought this was an appropriate solution. It was approved by the regional forester since they needed his approval for the large clear cuts. However, the plan was appealed, and the Washington office returned the plan for correction of shortcomings. By this time, I had moved on again and never had a chance to review the decision and their rationale. However, I do know that the Superior was the only forest I know of—and I was personally involved with twenty-three forest plans—where the supply of timber was far greater than the demand by industry. Those clear-cuts were not for timber but for moose.

We were fast approaching completion of our forest plans, and I needed to fill my old regional planner position. We had a meeting where a fellow from the Washington office planning staff stationed in Fort Collins, Colorado, gave us a briefing on what they were doing. His name was Don Meyer, and I was very impressed with him. I asked him if he might be interested in my old job, and he said he was very interested. It turns out he had some unpleasant experiences with the regional forester in Region 2 and was happy to leave Colorado. Don came in and didn't miss a beat. He did an excellent job, which made my job easier.

All the forests had about finished their plans except for the Hiawatha in Wisconsin. The forest planner there seemed to think he knew what to do but didn't. He was from out West and had been indoctrinated by the FORPLAN crowd. He didn't believe in what we were preaching and hadn't gotten off the first phase. We did everything we could to help him but without luck. Finally, Deputy Regional Forester Butch Maritta and I did a review of the forest. It was apparent the forest supervisor was not on top of the problem. We met with the rangers, and when asked they were not supportive of the forest planner. As one district ranger said, our biggest problem is not timber management, it's recreation management. The planner was engrossed in the FORPLAN model and totally disregarded the issues the forest faced. The district ranger who spoke up was Doug Glevanik. Before we left, Butch had the forest planner removed from the job and placed Doug in the forest planner's position. Within a couple of months Doug got on top of the planning process and completed the forest plan. He was promoted to the Clearwater National Forest in Region 1 as its forest planner, and several years later I hired him to be my assistant in Region 1 in Montana.

Tragedy Strikes

My kids were growing up and involved in school and soccer. Heidi was now 10 and Andrew 8. I had vacation time and took the whole family to Colorado to visit old friends and the places I used to work. We visited Gretchen's sister in Omaha and then went on to Denver. We stayed in Denver, and I took the kids to Mt. Evans and around the city. We then drove to Durango and took the narrow-gauge railroad to Silverton, Colorado, then on to my old hometown of Glenwood Springs and our friends Bob and Lois Veltus's home in the Roaring Fork Valley.

On the 4th of July 1984, they took us on a float trip down the Roaring Fork River. I had floated this river many times when I lived there in the early 1960s. It was a beautiful day, warm with sky-blue weather. They had had warm weather for a while, and the river was bank-full. Bob did some guiding and had all the gear and a large boat. Shortly after a streamside lunch we were floating along in rather calm water when we hit a rock that was slightly under the water. The boat suddenly flipped over, dumping all of us into the river. It was ice cold and moving fast. As I looked around I saw Gretchen and Heidi and we made it to shore, but I never saw Andrew. I learned later that when the raft tipped over, Andrew and Bob both ended up under it, so I could not see them. By then the raft, Bob, Lois, and Andrew were out of sight. I then saw Lois on the opposite bank. I panicked and ran to the nearest house. I said I needed a ride to the next bridge. The homeowner took me down a dirt road that would get me to the river. When I got there no one was in sight and I figured they had gone by. I again ran looking for someone to help, and that's when I saw Gretchen and Heidi. They had called the police and they were there to pick us up.

We drove into the city park just as they were loading Bob and Andrew in the ambulances. Lois joined us, and we followed one ambulance to the hospital. I was getting very angry as the ambulance in front of us with my son was stopping for red lights. The other ambulance was at the hospital when we arrived. I rushed in with Andrew, who was unconscious. They weren't going to let me into the emergency room, but I insisted. Andrew was regaining consciousness, but I worried that he might have some brain damage. I rushed out to tell Gretchen he was conscious but did not tell her what I thought. I wouldn't let her go back with me. When I arrived back, Andrew said, "Hi, Dad." It wasn't until I returned to the lobby that I saw Lois crying. Bob had died.

It turns out Bob and Andrew escaped from under the raft. Bob then put Andrew on his back with Andrew's arms through his life preserver. They went two miles downstream though class four and five rapids and could never make shore. There were several attempts to rescue them, but it wasn't until they had put rafts in at the park that they could grab them. Bob was already dead at that point, and Andrew was still holding on. His body temperature was eighty-four degrees, and he was almost gone as well.

That evening we all gathered at a friend's ranch and the Veltus family arrived. It was a sad event and I was still in shock. We took our kids back to Denver to stay with friends and went back for the funeral. Bob was buried on a hilltop overlooking the valley and the Roaring Fork River.

I wrote a letter to the Glenwood Springs *Daily Sentinel* thanking the community. I said, "Because of the combined efforts of residents, the police, paramedics, search and rescue, the Glenwood hospital staff, and Bob Veltus, my boy is alive and well. I give special thanks to my friend Bob, a hero who gave his life for Andrew."

Months later Bob was honored by the Carnegie Hero Fund Commission as the year's Carnegie Hero. It was a great honor for a great friend. The park where Andrew and Bob were pulled ashore was renamed Veltus Park in Bob's honor.

Glenwood Springs rafter, 57, gives up life to save boy, 8

By DAN MACARTHUR
Special to The Denver Post

GLENWOOD SPRINGS — A 57-year-old man gave his life to save a boy who fell into the chill Roaring Fork River in a Fourth of July rafting accident.

Robert Veltus, a Glenwood Springs businessman and former city councilman, was pronounced dead Wednesday at Valley View Hospital.

Veltus jumped into the river to save 8-year-old Andrew Hagamier of Brookfield, Wis., after the raft in which Veltus and the boy were riding overturned in rapids south of Glenwood Springs.

Upon reaching the boy, Veltus tied Andrew's life preserver to his own before losing consciousness.

The boy clung to Veltus' lifeless body, his arms tightly wrapped around his neck, for about 30 minutes before rescuers were able to pull them from the water.

"He saved that boy's life, no question about it," said Glenwood Springs police Lt. Don Williams. "It was a very brave thing to do."

"If (the Hagamier boy) hadn't had someone to hold onto, I don't think he would have made it," said Fred Perkes, director of the Glenwood Springs Ambulance Service. "I'm sure the kid would have given it up. Basically the guy put his life on the line to save the kid."

"I was amazed the boy was alive after that long in the water," Williams said. Williams said the boy's body temperature was 84 degrees when he was pulled from the river.

The boy was taken to Valley View Hospital, where he was treated for hypothermia and released.

Officials list the tentative cause of Veltus' death as drowning.

Glenwood Springs police said Veltus, his wife Lois, Mr. and Mrs. James Hagamier and their two children, a daughter who was unidentified and Andrew, were riding in a raft belonging to Veltus. All were wearing life preservers.

Police said the raft overturned just after noon Wednesday. All the adults made it safely to shore, but the children were seen floundering in the river. James Hagamier swam to his daughter and brought her ashore.

At about the same time, Veltus jumped in and swam to Andrew.

A rancher friend (standing), Bob (middle), and me hunting grouse on the Flattops in Colorado. Bob was like a father to me.

Page 2 — Glenwood Springs (Colo.) POST — Friday, July 27, 1984

Park renamed for Veltus

Kiwanis Park has been renamed "Veltus Park, A Kiwanian Project" in honor of Robert Veltus who died July 4 rescuing an 8-year-old boy from the Roaring Fork River.

Veltus, 57, and the boy, Andrew Hagameier, were riding in a raft along with Veltus' wife and Hagameier's sister and parents when it overturned in rapids south of town. All were able to make it to shore safely except the boy and his sister. Veltus jumped in and swam to the boy. The girl was rescued by her father.

Attorney John Schenk, his voice breaking with emotion, described the "supreme act of love" in which Veltus hooked onto the boy's life vest and held him above the icy water before being overcome and dying.

"His lifeless body became a refuge for that boy," Schenk said, describing how the boy held on to Veltus' body until being rescued nearly two miles downriver.

The Glenwood Springs City Council took the renaming action at Thursday's meeting.

CHAPTER 18

INTEGRATED
RESOURCE MANAGEMENT

Working together as a team

REGIONAL FORESTER Steve Yurick suddenly entered the hospital and had an operation for a growth on his lung. Fortunately, it was not cancer. Steve was a heavy smoker, and the incident shook him up. He immediately announced his retirement.

The new regional forester was Larry Henson, who was the present deputy regional forester. Larry had recently arrived in the region from Region 2 in Colorado and he and I had already had a disagreement.

We had a nursery in Minnesota and there was a question of whether it should be closed. I had concerns about its mission. They were primarily growing red pine. While I was on the Ottawa, the forest had a large acreage in red pine. There was no market for the timber. We were spending a lot of money growing trees that no one wanted. Rather than leap to a conclusion I asked Bill Shirley, the forester on my staff, to do an analysis of the costs and benefits of the nursery. His report showed the nursery indeed was not cost effective. Larry objected to the closing because of the social impacts to the employees and community— a worthy cause—but when your budget is limited you must make choices. Steve Yurick sided with me and closed the nursery. When Larry took over, he and I had a rocky start.

The region's fifteen forest plans were now complete, and we were now focused on how we would integrate our plans into our programming and budget process. Bob Jacobs was heading up that effort. Larry Henson was not particularly interested in the approach we were taking and expressed his disagreements to me.

About that time the chief of the Forest Service directed all the regions to come up with an approach on how they were going to implement their new forest plans. The next thing I knew Larry assigned me to head up a team to come up with a regionwide approach. He named Don Meyer to temporally take over my job as director.

Why he picked a staff director to lead the effort I did not know. Larry also named my team. Of the group, Ken Shalda, a forester in charge of timber sales, I thought was an excellent choice. The last three members I did not know well. Fred Hintasala, a civil engineer was a very quiet person. The other two were Bob Ratdke, a wildlife biologist, and Buz Durham, a landscape architect.

We Have a Story to Tell

None of our team had any idea where to start. We were in foreign country. The Forest Service we had all grown up in was driven by individual resource planning systems, such as timber or recreation planning. Multiple use planning was a catch phase, but not reality. There was very little or no integration. That was all left to the district rangers based on their perspective. Many of the resource values, such as wildlife, were considered not in an equal role but to mitigate the effects of other resource uses, again such as timber management. Even with forest plans that were supposedly integrated, when it got to implementation of those plans they were still driven by a functional project planning process.

How do we change this vision? We all asked, how do we change a culture built with its own individual successes over eighty years?

When we stated the task in these words, I suddenly felt like this was a great opportunity to at least start the process of change. Is this what our new regional forester really wanted?

When we framed the question to Larry he said, "Yes." Then the question was how?

I thought long and hard about what I had experienced during my career with the Forest Service and what I thought was missing from the way we did business. I kept coming back to the functional planning approach in which lip service was given to the other resources that might be affected. When I came to Region 9 from Region 2 they had a process in place I was intrigued with. They called it compartment analysis which is a smaller area of a ranger district. It was driven by timber planning, but they said they were considering all the resources together. This process had been accepted and used on all Region 9 national forests.

This analysis was done at the district level. On the Ottawa National Forest, the different district rangers and their primary staff would make a presentation of their findings to the forest supervisor and staff officers. I liked the concept. The focus was on unique ecosystems at a local level and included the involvement of local people. I was particularly impressed with a local approach to community involvement.

While Forest Supervisor Marv Lawerson focused on timber, I asked questions about local concerns and other resource values. Generally, my questions were answered by silence, except for a new district ranger by the name of Dick Brewster. Dick was near retirement, but still transferred to the Iron River District. He was not married and devoted to the Forest Service. When it was his district's turn to present their compartment analysis, I asked my questions. Dick went into detail on the people he contacted, and the type of balanced resource actions selected to address his resource and public concerns.

I recommended to our regional office team we build on this

system to use as a model for implementing our new forest plans. The forests knew the basics of how the system was applied and hopefully would understand how we intended to expand on it. Our team bought into the concept and we were off and running. The results ended up the being called "integrated resource management."

From Functional Planning to Integration

We broke the system into phases. The first phase was to identify "Opportunity Areas." These areas were subparts of a ranger district comprising unique ecosystems and local communities that had a direct relationship to the area being planned.

The second phase was to see how the area could contribute to the goals in their forest plan. If the planning staff had done their job there should be information on the forest plans concerns associated with these areas. The district would then talk, and if needed meet, with community members and determine their current concerns or where they might contribute. This effort would lead to more site-specific analysis.

Based on these findings the district staff, with additional expertise from the forest supervisor's office, or other sources, would do a more detailed analysis. The result would be a list of possible actions including projects, an implementation schedule and further design needs.

Incorporated into all these efforts should be the concept of community involvement and monitoring to determine a need to change the forest plan.

Everyone in the Forest Service knows what these terms mean but, in my mind, they didn't go far enough in applying them.

During the forest planning process, public involvement became an impersonal process conducted by a team that had very little knowledge of the people and cultures they were communicating with. In many cases the person with the most knowledge, the local district ranger, was left out of the process. Meetings and postcards were the primary means of "talking with people." Although some of these techniques are needed, I felt the information should be based on the local community needs and wants, and then built upward. If you've lost everyday contact with your neighbors, you lose their support and trust. In our IRM process we emphasized being good neighbors by getting to know our neighbors better, understanding how to reach them in an informal manner, and giving them opportunities to express their needs and learn to understand our limitations. We must respect their feelings and opinions and continue to maintain communications with them, like any good neighbor, on a day-to-day basis.

With community involvement, all types of opportunities can surface. I can remember on the Bessemer District of the Ottawa, where the district ranger partnered with the county to provide a winter supply of wood to senior citizens in need. The district provided the wood though a thinning project, the various groups in the community provided the labor, and the county delivered the wood with their road maintenance trucks. There are all kinds of shared efforts that could be generated.

We also wanted to make it an ongoing approach to identify possible amendments to the forest plan based on the evaluation of management direction needed on each management area. This might include boundary changes and modification of management direction goals and standards. Most important is talking with your neighbors and other publics to determine a need to change, as well as carrying out the forest plan's intent.

The team agreed with the approach. We then decided on how we wanted to communicate it to our organization. We felt we needed a field staff on our team to present it to the region—preferably a district ranger with credibility. I recommended the district ranger who had given me the idea, Dick Brewster from the Iron River District on the Ottawa National Forest. I approached Dick with the concept, and he said he would do it and even had an ongoing area analysis he could use to test the concept.

We Need to Be Together

We developed a brochure and a visual presentation and proposed we have an all-district ranger meeting to make the presentation. The meeting would also include outside instructors on issues such as improving our relationship with our neighbors. We were able to contract with Gifford Pinchot III to begin the session talking about his grandfather Gifford Pinchot, the first chief of the Forest Service and his principles. Larry Henson approved our strategy and went one step further. He wanted to go to each national forest in Region 9 and present it to all our employees and be personally involved by giving the keynote address. We now had a logistical nightmare, but we made it work.

It was a wonderful experience to visit every forest and get to meet many different folks from West Virginia to the north woods of Minnesota.

By now my doubts about my team were gone. Everyone pitched in and took the job they were best at. It was one of the highlights of my career to see the team work and the results. The region embraced the process and implemented it. Years later I had forest supervisors who had been district rangers in Region 9 come up to me and say how much the approach had improved their ability to foster resource integration on their units.

In 1992, six years after I left Region 9, I got a certificate of appreciation from the Eastern Region leadership team for, "major contributions toward setting the stage for the Eastern Region changing culture. Thank you for having been a significant player on the team." I had received a number of rewards in my career for individual effort, but this certificate resulted from a team effort. I have always been critical of the Forest Service for saying they are a multiple-use agency, but not practicing that philosophy in their planning. The Eastern Region embraced an integrated approach to multiple-use planning that I am proud to have played a role in.

Our team and Larry also gave our presentation to the chief and Washington office staff as well as a national timber manager meeting in Atlanta, Georgia. The meeting with the chief went well. In Atlanta, Larry talked to the timber managers about how we needed to change our approach to timber planning in the Forest Service. That message was not well received.

As a result of all that we went through, Larry and I found we shared common values and became good friends. I was looking forward to being able to implement what we had put together when Larry informed me that he was moving to the Washington as a new assistant deputy chief for resource management. He didn't want to go, but the chief said he needed someone to fill his shoes if a Democrat was elected president. But George Bush was elected, and Larry spent the next several years sitting in the corner until he could become the Region 3 regional forester. Sadly, Larry was diagnosed with lung cancer and retired. I was able to visit Larry at his home in Las Vegas and keep in touch with him until he passed away.

After Larry moved to Washington, I got a call from my former boss on the Black Hills National Forest, Jim Overbay. Jim was now the regional forester in Region 1, comprising Idaho,

Montana and North Dakota. He asked me whether I would be interested in the job of director of planning, programming, and budgeting for the region. The job was now included with management systems, run by Jim Reid. He felt the job had gotten too big for one director and wanted to split the duties. This caught me by surprise as it appeared to me my next move was to Washington. My children were now 10 and 13 and to move to a place like Missoula, Montana would be great. I still had great memories of Montana and Missoula from my smokejumping days and couldn't believe we could move there. Gretchen was not so sure. She liked Milwaukee.

I told Jim I would be interested, but I didn't think Washington would go for it. He said, "Leave it to me." It wasn't long, and the move was approved. Gretchen and I flew to Missoula and began house-hunting.

CHAPTER 19

NORTHERN REGION
BIG SKY COUNTRY

Missoula Valley and the Bitterroot Range

Photo taken from my home in Missoula

I HAD JUST MOVED to Montana when Jim Overbay had a management team meeting with staff directors and forest supervisors. I was introduced and sat back and listened. I was taken back at the put downs and general attitude of the group. After six years in Region 9, I had gotten spoiled with the teamwork and willingness to work together on differences. The meeting reminded me of the days in Region 2, with the same negative atmosphere.

After the meeting, Jim asked my opinion of the discussion, and I told him my feelings. He had been in Region 1 about one year and said he agreed with me. He opened the issue to the other directors. They also agreed and said they were willing to try to change. Jim hired a consultant to work with the management team, which resulted in a series of meetings to talk over the issues and make some changes. While the meetings helped, they never did resolve all the problems. I felt the communications between the staff directors improved but there will still conflicts with some forest supervisors.

My new job proved to be another set of challenges. We still had several forest plans that needed to be finalized. Most were between draft and final and there was intense political and public controversy—in particular, the level of proposed timber harvest. The timber industry was under pressure on several fronts. Most of the smaller operators had mills that were over thirty years old and needed substantial investments to modernize. Thus, they needed the timber supply to be as high as it had been in the past or even more to justify the cost to upgrade their facilities.

The forest planning process had shown that most of the available timber supply had already been cut or was now constrained by other values or the results of adjacent harvest on private lands. The planners were forced to look to marginal lands or roadless areas with very high costs to maintain old harvest levels. The FORPLAN linear program had shown the timber was there but the results were over-optimistic.

The first job my boss asked me to do was evaluate the Bitterroot National Forest Plan and the process. The draft plan was available for public review and the proposed alternative had a harvest level below what they had traditionally accomplished. They were under pressure to maintain or increase the output. I met with the planners and with the district rangers. The rangers, after ground checking the preferred alternative, said they couldn't meet the proposed harvest level in year one let alone over a ten-year period. The problem was the draft forest plan had alternatives with higher harvest levels, which meant they were infeasible. The planning regulations required that all alternatives must be feasible.

I reported my findings back to Jim Overbay, and he said he feared as much. The question to me was, what do we do? There were only two choices, start the planning process over or move forward with the present preferred alternative and spell out the reason for shortfall in the harvest levels through the required monitoring and evaluation process. Jim said he couldn't have them start over as the organizational and financial costs were too high, so he favored allowing the proposed plan to be released to the public as a final document. He then asked me to do a quick review of the other pending draft plans and see if their situations were similar. It turned out they were similar, but their preferred alternatives were more realistic. How wrong I was. A few years later most of the region's national forests with big timber programs said their harvest levels were too high.

Their solution was to redo their forest plans. Not because their plans limited them from doing the best they could but because they were under criticism from the public.

I held my ground against redoing the plans. The costs to the organization and our employees were too high in my opinion. I took a lot of heat and may have made some enemies. This all played out over several years. Overbay moved to Washington and our new Regional Forester, John Muma, had come and gone. Dave Jolly took his place and the arguments continued. I still advocated the monitoring and evaluation solution, but only the forests in the eastern part of Montana supported that approach.

Top-down Planning to Extremes

Then the Democrats under Bill Clinton took office, and overnight the program changed. With the advent of the spotted owl lawsuit, the "President's Plan" shut down the timber program in most of Region 6—Oregon and Washington. Then the Washington office, under the direction of the Secretary of Agriculture, embarked on the "Columbia River Basin Plan" affecting all the forest plans in the rest of Oregon and Washington and a number of forests in Idaho and Montana. This effort would have changed all the plans in a similar manner.

I have never advocated top-down planning. Even the forest planning process, I felt, was too top down. I always advocated planning at a local level considering the unique natural and social conditions and then bringing the results together to provide a forest wide perspective. Now we were headed in the opposite direction. It became a my-way-or-the-highway approach, and if you voiced any displeasure you could look for another job. My regional forester, Dave Jolly, expressed concern over how public involvement was being done at a coordination meeting. After our lunch break he got called out of the meeting and read the riot act by the secretary's office in Washington. Although I did my best to stay positive and support the effort, I felt we were headed in the wrong direction. It was time to retire and I did in January of 1995. Dave Jolly followed me three months later. When President Bush took office, the whole effort—including the millions of dollars spent on the basin plan—was thrown out.

See You in Court

During my time in Montana and Region 1 of the Forest Service, I witnessed and was part of some significant changes that have altered the course of the organization forever. The most significant was the relationship of federal regulations and the court system. In the Forest Service's case, it was driven by three laws, the National Environmental Policy Act, the Endangered Species Act, and the National Forest Management Act. All of these acts were passed in the 1970s. In the latter two, the acts were followed by regulations. In the case of the National Environmental Policy Act there were very few regulations. As a result, judges created the rules through their rulings.

I was most familiar with planning regulations that were developed after the National Forest Management Act was passed. The regulations were developed by a team of scientists. They were well-meaning but in some cases the requirements were more theory than fact and impossible to meet, especially by a vast number of units. The regulations for these acts were prime fodder for individuals smart enough to challenge the results in court. If the judges ruled against the organization, the results were new rules, like regulations, that applied to every project being worked on, causing everything to stop until the projects could be redone. Some courts were more aggressive than others and the plaintiffs sought those courts out for their lawsuits.

Unfortunately, Montana was one of the top states being challenged by a variety of groups and they found a judge who was willing to justify changes to many of our decisions. Our people were totally unprepared for this type of workload. They were not lawyers but land management specialists. While they knew resource issues they did not know how to play the legal game. My staff had the responsibility to provide the support needed to address the legal issues that arose. When this all started, I had one staff person with that job, by the time I retired I had about twenty.

The Forest Service could not hire lawyers. That job was supposed to be handled by the Department of Justice, with the Office of General Council providing legal assistance. They were understaffed and could not help our field people. I started combing the countryside for lawyers with a natural resource background who would be interested in working for the Forest Service. I was able to find four. They were all outstanding people and understood the issues. We created what we called our "coach approach." These folks would go out to the forests with other staff to assist and provide guidance and recommendations. The forests also increased their staffs to meet the need. While successful in improving our planning and project disclosure documents under the National Environmental Policy Act (NEPA), it was an ongoing battle and still exists today at an extremely high cost.

All these issues led to a substantial decrease in the number of lumber mills. Most could not afford to modernize their mills and we were not able to provide a steady flow of timber sales. Congress soon decreased our funding in timber management, which had been a major contributor to our fixed costs such as offices etc., so the funds available to other resource programs had to carry the costs.

At the same time a couple of environmental groups, fully understanding that they had us on the ropes from a legal standpoint, were making noise about shutting down our grazing program. Most grazing allotments and permits were put in place decades before but as they came up for renewal they needed to comply with NEPA and the Endangered Species Act. We were more behind on grazing than on timber sales from a legal standpoint.

I was asked by the law school at the University of Montana to talk about the grazing issue and what we were doing to comply with the law. What I talked about was the federal budget system in relationship to the grazing program. Congress gave the Forest Service very little in the way of funds to run and maintain a viable program. From my experience that was by design. The fewer dollars we had the less we would interfere with the grazing permittees. Our ability to identify resource problems was limited, making it harder to improve the range conditions. That was not what the lawyers wanted to hear. They envisioned a discussion on how we would comply with all the laws.

Where we had willing permittees we got by, where we had bad ones the land suffered. The National Wildlife Association started putting pressure on us to comply with these laws, but we were limited by dollars. As a result, our only recourse was to shut the grazing program down. Congress now went ballistic. This was like the feds shutting down the American cowboy. Suddenly there were laws proposed that would give the permitted users a "private right" for their cattle numbers. If that act passed the federal treasury would have to buy the permittees cows, if we, or the courts, reduced the permit numbers. The National Wildlife Association quit pursuing its strategy.

The grazing industry was one of the user groups that most opposed the creation of the National Forest System. They were finally won over but many in their industry felt they had a vested right to free grazing on public lands and were bitter over the final decision. That belief has persisted ever since and occasionally has erupted in a cry to have the land given to the states or sold to the private sector.

The issue of how the National Forests were to be managed was now in the public agenda, from selling the land, to challenging the Forest Service in court over decisions that effected individual public desires. These constant legal challenges were sufficient to halt project work as some unspoken strategy. This all started in earnest in the 1990s and to a certain extent still exists today. I can't help but believe that one of the frustrations by local people that rely on the Forest Service to meet their multiple use mandate has caused many to want federal lands handed over to the states or sold. From both a national level and a local level, this would be a serious disruption of the functioning of a community and society. Much of these lands are lands that nobody wanted, steep, rugged, inaccessible and difficult to manage. The costs to county residences would far surpass the property taxes or other resource benefits they could generate. One major fire alone, which always happens suddenly, would overwhelm a county's fire protection capability and leave it bankrupt. That's exactly how the national forests in the Eastern part of the country were created. Homesteaders settled the land but couldn't make a living on it. They walked away leaving counties to cope with decreased tax revenue and saddled with the cost of management, such as fire control. Congress then passed the Weeks Act to purchase the lands to be administered by the U.S. Forest Service. In many cases the greatest economic and social value of these lands is for all the public to use and enjoy them and the only viable management strategy is for all citizens to share in the cost.

When I became a district ranger, I became aware of just how important the forest was to the community. It took many forms from economic to social to spiritual. I believe the district ranger's most important job is to know the community and how it functions and to provide ways of supporting it.

When we developed our approach to implementing our new forest plans in Region 9, we emphasized getting to know our neighbors. That became one of the main principles in the region. While it was forest plan implementation, my hope was that it would become a way of life for all our activities. That approach was successful for decades.

I must admit, in the later part of my career I was in regional headquarters, and except for field reviews, I didn't have the joy of working with field people and local publics, which I loved. Politics dominated, and with every different administration and its party, they tried to remake the Forest Service in their image. So, I drifted into retirement and tried my hand at consulting, but found it was just like what I had done in my job. I then started to volunteer with the National Smokejumpers Association. They had started a program to assist the Forest Service by working on forest projects (a repayment for all they gave us as young men and women as we found our way in life). I can recall many experiences after retirement that were rewarding but this was one of the best.

Several years after we started our volunteer efforts, the Helena National Forest asked our group to help them with some trail work and other jobs at Mann Gulch, where thirteen young smokejumpers lost their life to a forest fire in 1949. Since that time this valley has had significant meaning to our members and to many people in the firefighting community as well as a designation as a National Historic site. Norman McLean wrote his book *Young Men and Fire* about this incident.

To get to Mann Gulch you normally must go by boat. It lies in the middle of Holder Reservoir outside of Helena, Montana. You must have a boat or ride on a tour boat from the end of the lake to get there. Our crew of fourteen former smokejumpers took our own boats to Meriwether boat site one drainage south of Mann Gulch. It was a beautiful day and trip through the Gates of the Rockies Canyon, long ago described by Lewis and Clark. Unfortunately, the next morning a spring storm set in. It snowed and rained on our expedition.

Our crew split up with ten jumpers working on a trail and other projects. Four of us were going to hike into Mann Gulch and take GPS readings of where each smokejumper who died had dropped. Roy Williams and Roger Savage hiked into the area from the top of the gulch while Carl Gidlund and I got a boat ride to the base of the gulch and hiked up from there. As Carl and I hiked up the steep incline the weather became more intense. Carl was not dressed for the conditions and was starting to have problems. He stopped to rest, and I went ahead and joined Roy and Roger. When the job was done I thought I had better get back to Carl. When I arrived, he was beginning to show signs of hypothermia and shaking. We immediately headed for the lake, and when there I tried to light a fire. I couldn't, too wet. Our boat ride back to camp wasn't to arrive for another couple hours. With the canyon cliffs there was no way we could hike out. I was beginning to panic.

We were huddled under a large fir tree trying to stay somewhat dry. Just then a tour boat came around the bend and without thinking I ran to the lakeshore and yelled for help. They pulled over and asked what the problem was, I said my partner is going into shock from hypothermia—a lie—but he was close. The boat was filled with teachers and students and the teachers, mostly women, jumped into action. They embraced Carl and immediately started to strip his wet clothes off and hugged him to warm him up. Carl had this shocked look on his face, and then, as I talked to the captain, a big grin.

I was having fun again.

Former smokejumpers at the Mann Gulch Memorial
Carl Gidlund is leaning on the sculpture

CHAPTER 20

MY ULTIMATE GOAL

Jewel Basin, Montana, on my 80th birthday
With my children, Heidi and Andrew

MOST OF THE JOBS I had with the Forest Service were either offered to me or ones I was directed to take. I was lucky to like them all even though they were all different challenges. My very best job in the Forest Service was as the district ranger on the Dillon District of the Arapaho National Forest in Colorado. My last job, thanks to Jim Overbay, the regional forester in the Northern Region, was in many respects the most important, moving to Missoula, Montana. Not from a work standpoint but for my family and me personally. My personal goals changed as the years went by from trying to make a difference as a landscape architect, to becoming a forest supervisor, to doing the most for my family. That became my ultimate goal.

My wife Gretchen was finally able to settle down into a job teaching children, which she so enjoyed—though it was not an easy trip for her. When we married, she had a wonderful job as a first-grade teacher in Cherry Creek School District in Colorado, which she had to quit when we moved. She ran a day care and preschool center in Dillon, Colorado, then a preschool in Brookfield, Wisconsin. When she arrived in Missoula, there were no jobs available, so even with a master's degree she had to go back to the University of Montana for a special education certificate to get a job. She then taught special education for ten years in Alberton, Montana, before retirement. Alberton was tough, a forty-mile drive away and a community that had a number of underprivileged students with severe handicaps. Still, she enjoyed the job and the people.

Two Great Kids

Our kids Heidi and Andrew were thirteen and ten when we moved to Missoula from Wisconsin. I knew the town well, but they were a bit apprehensive. All the way to Missoula they dialed the radio trying to find music that met their tastes, with no luck. As we came down Hellgate Canyon, outside of town, they finally hit the right channel.

We had bought a house that was about five miles from town, up the Rattlesnake Valley on a mountainside. Gretchen was worried that our kids wouldn't have anyone to play with. That was hardly the case. The boy next door, Matt Graf, became Andrew's lifelong friend. There were two other girls in Heidi's class in the neighborhood. We belonged to a neighborhood pool and had great neighbors.

Heidi turned into quite a young lady. Smart and forceful. Sometimes hard to handle. She was very athletic and excelled in soccer. Both our kids had started soccer while in Brookfield, Wisconsin. They had a great program so when we moved to Montana they were way ahead in soccer skills. Andrew played on a neighborhood team with all his buddies for many years and went on to play varsity soccer at Hellgate High for four years. They didn't have girls' soccer at that time and Heidi played on a mixed team along with Courtney Torgerson, our neighbor. Her senior year in high school was the first year they started girls' soccer in Montana. Both she and Courtney made all-state.

Heidi also got her mother's smarts and excelled in school. Her senior year she was selected from a statewide contest to represent Montana at a nationwide convention in Minnesota. She then went to the University of Wisconsin and majored in journalism. She was offered great jobs in the Midwest, but Montana kept calling and she ended up as a cub reporter in Livingston, Montana.

Always an outdoor girl, she was drawn to the adventures and life in and around Yellowstone Park. While there she was invited by the National Park Service to visit and write about the wolves that were soon to be released into the wild. After a short stint with the Bozeman, Montana, newspaper she quit and spent the next six months backpacking in New Zealand. Heidi finally settled down as a reporter and then city editor for the Bend Bulletin in Oregon. After another adventure of two years in Bern, Switzerland, with her husband Tim Neville and new baby Evie Neville, she became the communications director for the Oregon Natural Desert Association and then the High Desert Museum in Bend, Oregon.

Andrew's path was different. I raised him to be self-reliant. Every Memorial Day and Labor Day he and I would go fishing or hunting and camp out in the forest. He and his buddies were always playing war games and running the mountain behind our house. I still find old fox holes dug over twenty years ago. Paintball games were a weekend affair. Dressed all in camouflage with paint smudges on their uniforms and faces, they roamed the forests. Even the deer in our neighborhood weren't safe. They were dressed in multicolored paint. More than once sirens would rouse us from one of their campfires escaping or a gas line being dug up. While his school grades were average, his outdoor skills increased from his first turkey to his first deer.

The highlight of his outdoor education came at seventeen. Through my Forest Service contacts on the Flathead National Forest, I called Al Ross, the Spotted Bear assistant ranger, to see if they had a spot on his district for Andrew and his friend Matt Graf to work as volunteers. He said he did. I drove them up to Hungry Horse, Montana, then down fifty miles of gravel road to the Spotted Bear Ranger District. It's the portal to the Bob Marshall Wilderness Area, one of the wildest areas in the country. I dropped them off at the trailhead with their backpacks and instructions to follow the trail to Bear Creek Guard Station, where they would rendezvous with all the district's crews for training. My last advice was watch out for grizzly bears.

As I returned home it started to rain and for the next two weeks it poured. I was worried, but I bought Andrew a good sleeping bag that would keep him warm even if it got wet. Almost fifty years before I had packed into the Mount of the Holy Cross Wilderness in Colorado and got caught in a severe rain and snowstorm. My new down sleeping bag got soaked and I came close to freezing to death.

When I returned to Spotted Bear, I found two young men hardened by their experience, full of stories and not one piece of clothing that was dry. It turns out they and one other crew spent the entire time working trails in the backcountry with a broken-down old mule and a cranky llama. What were normally ankle-deep creek crossings were up to their waists. They still tell stories, especially about the boar grizzly they encountered.

Both Andrew and Matt stayed with the Forest Service during their college summers and afterwards. Matt stayed in the Bob Marshall on trail crews, then on an interregional fire crew. Andrew spent the next six years as a sawyer cutting trees and on a fire crew in the Big Hole of Montana. Both got degrees in forestry, but there were no jobs available. Andrew got whatever job he could during the winter. He worked at Snowbowl Ski Area as a cook during the day and as a waiter in the evening. He then moved on to Boston working construction. One day he called to say he was going back to college to get a master's degree in land use planning. He graduated from the University of Arizona and since then has worked in both the private and public sector. He now works for Missoula County as a long-range planner.

After retirement I went to several retiree meetings. All they did was complain about the Forest Service. Times had changed and I moved away from the organization for many years. I started exploring Montana and Arizona while hunting and fishing with my good friend Bob Torgerson, but I didn't forget my love for the mountains and the mission of the organization. I volunteered every summer for fifteen years with the National Smokejumpers Association trails program. It gave me satisfaction and I met many new friends who shared my love of the forests.

As I now look back at all my experiences, I find I enjoyed living in wonderful places and meeting people from all walks of life. I have had the opportunity to do a wide variety of jobs—digging fire lines, backpacking Wilderness, designing facilities, managing forests and people, and serving my country.

I can no longer swing a Pulaski, but I can still dream of the days when I could. And I have the satisfaction of knowing my children will carry on this love for the forests.

Made in the USA
Columbia, SC
24 July 2020